Twayne's World Authors Series No. 769

0-8057-6620-0 $17.95

Pablo Neruda, Chilean poet, diplomat,
communist party leader, together with
Jorge Luis Borges and Gabriel García
Márquez, helped shape contemporary
Latin American literature and bring it to
the attention of both East and West. A surrealist, Neruda revitalized everyday language and employed bold metaphors in
free verse. Filled with love, grief, and despair, his poems celebrate the dramatic
Chilean landscape and rage against political
exploitation, particularly of the Indian.
His published work spanning sixty years,
Neruda served all over the world in the
consular service from 1927 on, received
the Nobel Prize for literature in 1971, and
died in Chile during the 1973 military
coup that toppled Salvador Allende's
socialist government.

In her lucid examination of Neruda's
best-known works, *Twenty Love Poems
and a Song of Despair, Residence on Earth,
Passions and Impressions,* and *Toward the
Splendid City: Nobel Lecture,* Marjorie Agosin
probes the vital connection between the
poet's life and work over six decades. To an
interpretive synthesis of readings by other
critics Agosin adds observations on form,
content, and the forces of instinct and
intuition that animate Neruda's highly personal style. Complete with chronology
and bibliography, this insightful study,
translated from the original Spanish by
Lorraine Roses, will enlighten seasoned
scholars, students and general readers alike.

59

PABLO NERUDA
(1904–1973)
Photograph courtesy of Matilde Urrutia

Pablo Neruda

By Marjorie Agosin
Wellesley College

Translated by Lorraine Roses

Twayne Publishers • Boston

Pablo Neruda

Marjorie Agosin

Copyright © 1986 by G. K. Hall & Co.
All Rights Reserved
Published by Twayne Publishers
A Division of G. K. Hall & Co.
70 Lincoln Street
Boston, Massachusetts 02111

Copyediting supervised by Lewis DeSimone
Book production by Lyda E. Kuth
Book design by Barbara Anderson

Typeset in 11 pt. Garamond
by Modern Graphics, Inc., Weymouth, Massachusetts

Printed on permanent/durable acid-free
paper and bound in the United States of
America

Library of Congress Cataloging in Publication Data

Agosin, Marjorie.
  Pablo Neruda.

  (Twayne's world authors series ; TWAS 769, Latin
American literature)
  Translated from the Spanish.
  Bibliography: p. 144
  Includes index.
  1. Neruda, Pablo, 1904–1973—Criticism and
interpretation.   I. Title.   II. Series: Twayne's world authors series ; TWAS
769.   III. Series: Twayne's world authors series. Latin American literature.
PQ8097.N4Z546   1986   861   85–21928
ISBN 0–8057–6620–0

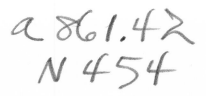
This book is dedicated to a free Chile.

Contents

About the Author

Marjorie Agosin is an assistant professor of Latin American literature at Wellesley College. She received the Ph.D. in Spanish from Indiana University in 1982. A Chilean poet and literary critic, Professor Agosin has published four collections of poetry. Her most recent collection, *Witches and Other Things (Brujas y algo más)*, was published by the Latin American Literary Review Press in 1984 in a bilingual edition translated by Cola Franzen.

Professor Agosin has written extensively on contemporary Chilean literature and culture; her essays have appeared in the United States, Europe, and Latin America. She is a contributor of a chapter on the Chilean woman for the international anthology *Sisterhood Is Global* (Doubleday, 1984), edited by Robin Morgan. She is also the author of a critical study dedicated to the novelist Maria Luisa Bombal, *Las desterradas del paraiso* (Senda Nueva de Ediciones, 1983), and a contributor for Scribner's Latin American author series.

About the Translator

Lorraine Elena Roses studied at Mount Holyoke College, the University of Puerto Rico, and Harvard University, where she received the Ph.D. She is the author of *Voices of a Storyteller: Cuba's Lino Novás Calvo* (Greenwood Press, 1986), and numerous articles, reviews, and translations of Latin American literature published in the *Revista de Estudios Hispanicos*, *Latin American Literary Review*, *Symposium*, *Chasqui*, *Studies in Afro-Hispanic Literature*, *Discurso Literario*, and other journals. She is an associate professor of Spanish at Wellesley College.

Preface

Pablo Neruda is a name, a phenomenon, a presence in world literature requiring no introduction. During half a century of literary labor, he produced over thirty books of poetry, two of prose, and even a book of recipes, the latter written in collaboration with Miguel Angel Asturias, another winner of the Nobel Prize for literature from Latin America. Neruda was awarded the prize in 1971. Two years later, the year of his untimely death, the publishing house of Losada in Buenos Aires printed his complete works in three weighty volumes of some three thousand pages that include most, but not all, of his poetry, theater, and essays. Since that time eight books have been published posthumously.

Neruda's impact on Latin American literature cannot be overemphasized. For it was he, more than any other writer, who began in the early 1920s to bring Latin American literature to the attention of the international community. It is very difficult to comprehend the phenomenon of Neruda, for in addition to being a prolific, serious, and innovative writer, he was also, like Cervantes, a popular writer.

The newcomer to Neruda may very well feel overwhelmed by the sheer volume of his production. Therefore, one of my most difficult considerations for this study was simply that of selection. I decided to use the limited space to concentrate on the most fundamental works of Neruda, and my discussion of these works is organized around the recurring themes of his poetry: love, nature, justice, the American continent, and Latin America in particular: its physiography, identity, and destiny. These themes have been dealt with on an equal plane of importance and analysis and are offered as keys to the complexity and variety in the poetry of the very Chilean and very international poet, Pablo Neruda.

I have attempted to indicate how each theme evolves and is organically linked to the preceding phase. As an example, all the love poetry is grouped in one chapter. Here we may observe the evolution of a young man alienated from his surroundings seeking union with a beloved woman, then turning into the mature man who after tribulations and disappointments ultimately finds fulfillment.

Each chapter includes a discussion of the books that have had the greatest impact and significance in two directions: within the poetry of Neruda himself and in that of Latin America as a whole. The reader will find here the essential and basic Neruda, the Neruda who manifests his own life in his books. For the events in the poet's life are inextricably linked to his lyrical production. His experience in the Far East gave rise to the *Residence on Earth* and his experience in Spain during the Civil War, which determined his adhesion to a Marxist political philosophy, turned him toward his own continent, Latin America, and in the subsequent book, *Canto general,* caused him to search for a new and apt poetic language. I hope the bibliography at the end of the book will serve as an orientation so that the reader may continue exploring and enjoying Neruda beyond this brief study.

I am grateful to the many critics who have studied Neruda's poetry so assiduously. The ideas in this book have been stimulated by their work and represent a synthesis and integral vision of the man and the poet, showing both the constancy and change involved in the practice of his art. I have not omitted the political aspects of Neruda's work, because they are equal and essential parts of one being, one art.

The studies of Neruda are as abundant as his own production. Therefore this book is based on those that I personally have found most useful, for example, *Earth Tones* by Margery Safir and Manuel Durán. Because of limitations of space it has been impossible to analyze in more detail some important segments of the poetry, but in those cases I have pointed out specific poems for further analysis.

Neruda, unlike fellow poets such as Mistral and Paz, has left no reflections on his own work, for he approached poetry in an intuitive and almost mystical fashion. This book has attempted to capture the freedon-loving and joyous spirit of Neruda, which cannot be categorized or pigeonholed but is ever ready to delight and inspire the reader who will agree to travel along with him.

Marjorie Agosin

Wellesley College

Acknowledgments

I am grateful to my colleagues in the Spanish Department of Wellesley College for their support and encouragement during the writing of this book.

My great appreciation also goes to Cola Franzen for her dedication and her perceptive reading of the manuscript; to Naomi Lindstrom for her continuous encouragement throughout my career; to David William Foster for his editorial help and guidance; and to Nancy Schena for all those late hours at the computer deciphering those impossible footnotes.

Matilde Urrutia deserves recognition for sharing with me her personal vision of her husband Pablo Neruda—a vision that I had already intuited thanks to my mother, Frida Agosín, who took me to Isla Negra during my childhood. It was there that I found the beauty and energy of Neruda's poetry before I was able to read it.

Finally, I wish to thank John Wiggins, my husband, for his love, patience, and constant belief in my work.

About the Author

Marjorie Agosin is an assistant professor of Latin American literature at Wellesley College. A native of Chile, she is a literary critic and the author of four volumes of poetry, including *Brujas y algo mas (Witches and Other Things)*.

About the Translator

Lorraine Roses is an associate professor of Spanish at Wellesley College and the author of *Voices of a Storyteller: Cuba's Lino Novás Calvo*.

Chronology

1904   12 July, Ricardo Eliecer Neftalí Reyes is born in Parral, Chile.

1919   Wins third prize in the poetry competition, "Los juegos florales del Maule," with his poem "Nocturno ideal" and the next year adopts the pseudonym Pablo Neruda.

1921   Travels to the capital to study to be a French teacher. His poem "La canción de la fiesta" wins first prize in a poetry competition held by the Student Organization of the University of Chile.

1923   First edition of *Crepusculario.*

1924   First edition of *Veinte poemas de amor y una cancion desesperada* (*Twenty Love Poems and a Song of Despair*).

1926   First edition of *El habitante y su esperanza* (The inhabitant and his hope).

1927   Travels to Rangoon as honorary consul of Chile, stopping at Buenos Aires, Rio de Janeiro, Lisbon, Madrid, Port Said, Djibouti, Colombo, Singapore, Bangkok, Shanghai, and Tokyo.

1928   Consul in Colombo, Ceylon.

1930   Consul in Batavia, Java. Marries Maria Antonieta Hagenaar.

1931   Consul in Singapore.

1932   Returns to Chile.

1933   First edition of *El hondero entusiasta* (The ardent slingsman). In August appointed Chilean consul to Buenos Aires. Lives there with his wife, sharing their apartment with the Chilean author María Luisa Bombal.

1934   Appointed consul to Barcelona and then Madrid. His only child, Malva Marina, is born in Madrid.

1935   Meets the painter Delia del Carril, who would become his second wife. *Residencia en la tierra (Residence on Earth)* is published in two volumes in Madrid.

1936   García Lorca dies in Granada. Neruda begins to write *España en el corazón (Spain in My Heart)*. Divorces Maria Antonieta Hagenaar.

1937   *Spain in My Heart* is published in Chile.

1939   Consul in Paris, also working at headquarters of agency dealing with Spanish immigration to Chile. *Las furias y las penas (The Furies and the Sorrows)* is published.

1940   16 August, named Chile's consul general in Mexico.

1942   His daughter dies in Holland.

1945   Elected senator in Chile's presidential elections on 4 March. Wins National Prize for Literature in May. Joins Chilean Communist party.

1947   First edition of *Tercera residencia (The Third Residence)*, which includes *The Furies and the Sorrows* and *Spain in My Heart*.

1950   3 April, first edition of *Canto general* is published in Mexico City. 22 November, receives the Peace Prize in Warsaw.

1953   January. Travels to the Soviet Union to receive the Lenin Peace Prize.

1955   Separates from Delia del Carril and moves to Santiago, where he lives with Matilde Urrutia.

1958   Publication of *Estravagaria (Extravagaria)* in Buenos Aires.

1959   Limited edition of *Cien sonetos de amor (One Hundred Love Sonnets)* in Buenos Aires.

1962   The Brazilian newspaper *O Cruzeiro Internacional* publishes "Las vidas del poeta: Memorias y reminicencias" in ten consecutive articles.

1964   National Library of Chile celebrates his sixtieth birthday. Five volume edition of *Memorial de Isla Negra (Isla Negra: A Notebook)* is published.

1965   February. Receives honorary doctorate from Oxford.

1966   Travels to the United States as guest of honor at a PEN Club meeting. He gives readings in New York and makes recordings for the Library of Congress. He writes the drama *Fulgor y muerte (Splendor and Death of Joaquin Murieta)*.

1967   Travels to Moscow. *Barcarola (Barcarole)* is published in Buenos Aires.

**Other critical studies on Latin American writers
in Twayne's World Authors Series include:**

Gabriel García Márquez	Raymond Williams
Jorge Luis Borges	Martin S. Stabb
Mario Vargas Llosa	Dick Gerdes
Juan Rulfo	Luis Leal
Alejo Carpentier	Donald Shaw
José Donoso	George R. McMurray
Juan José Arreola	Yulan M. Washburn
Lino Novás Calvo	Raymond D. Sousa
Clarice Lispector	Earl Fitz
José Revueltas	Sam L. Slick

1968   Made honorary member of the North American Academy of Arts and Letters and of the National Institute of Arts and Letters of Venezuela. Returns to Chile and begins to work with the journal *Ercilla* in Santiago (1968–70).

1969   September, the Senate of the Republic of Chile decorates him with the Silver Medal that is conferred upon Chile's distinguished sons. Presidential candidate of the Chilean Communist party.

1970   January, resigns his candidacy for president in order to designate someone from Chile's united leftist parties.

1971   Receives the Nobel Prize for literature.

1973   5 February, Neruda resigns as ambassador to Paris. 11 September, a new military government takes power in Chile. Salvador Allende dies. 23 September, Neruda dies of cancer in a Santiago Clinic.

1985   9 January, Matilde Urrutia dies of cancer.

Chapter One
The Chile of Pablo Neruda

One evocative passage in Pablo Neruda's memoirs reflects particularly the importance of natural surroundings and landscapes in his poetry. Chile, that long and narrow strip of land at the bottom of the map of South America, is embedded in his poetry, as it is in his heart:

Comenzaré por decir, sobre los días y años de mi infancia, que mi único personaje inolvidable fue la lluvia. La gran lluvia austral que cae como una catarata del Polo, desde los cielos del Cabo de Hornos hasta la frontera. En esta frontera o Far West de mi patria, nací a la vida, a la tierra, a la poesía y a la lluvia.

(I shall start out by saying this about the days and years of my childhood: the rain was the one unforgettable presence for me then. The great southern rain, coming down like a waterfall from the Pole, from the skies of Cape Horn to the frontier. On this frontier, my country's Wild West, I first opened my eyes to life, the land, poetry, and the rain.)[1]

To understand and visualize the poetry of Pablo Neruda, we must go back to those regions of the author's childhood,[2] where his poetry was born. The poet Pablo Neruda was born Ricardo Eliecer Neftalí Reyes Basoalto. He came into the world on 12 July 1902, in Parral, a small village in the central valley of Chile surrounded, as its name suggests, by abundant vineyards. His mother, Rosa Basoalto de Reyes, died of tuberculosis a month after her son was born. His father, José del Carmen Reyes, remarried in 1906 to Trinidad Candía, who was truly a second mother to the little boy. In his poetry he remembers her as a warm woman with a sense of humor and calls her affectionately *la mamadre,* or "second mother."

The young Neftalí remained only a short time in his native city, for the family, including his sister Laura and brother Rodolfo, moved south, to the city of Temuco. Neftalí lived in Temuco for the full fifteen years of his adolescence. He would always remember the luxuriant nature that surrounded him there—the forests, the rain, and the smell of freshly cut wood from the many sawmills. He would also recall the presence of a father both loved and feared. On occasion, this father, engineer of a freight train that scaled the Andean peaks, would take the young Neftalí on journeys along the railways of southern Chile, in the heavy rain of winter or the heat of summer.

It is important to remember that from an early age, contact with nature imprinted on the boy a special sensitivity and view of the world. The rain and the woods are two elements that took on a transcendental importance in his work. As he himself tells us in the poem "Primer viaje" ("The First Journey"):

> Del pecho polvoriento de mi patria
> me llevaron sin habla
> hasta la lluvia de la Araucanía
> las tablas de la casa
> olían a bosque,
> a selva pura.
> Desde entonces mi amor
> fue maderero.
>
> (From the dusty bosom of my country
> They took me, still an infant,
> into the rain of the Araucania.
> The boards of the house
> smelled of the woods,
> of the deep forest.
> From that time on, my love
> had wood in it.)[3]

Neftalí attended school at the Liceo de Temuco, whose head-mistress was Gabriela Mistral, the poet who in 1945 would win the first Nobel Prize for literature ever given to a Spanish American. It is a remarkable coincidence that these two noted poets should meet in the remote village of Temuco and that there Neftalí began, under the tutelage of Gabriela Mistral, his first readings of nineteenth-century Russian novelists, French symbolists, and especially the poetry of Verlaine.

In his memoirs the poet speaks of afternoons spent exploring the thick, leafy forests of the region, and, in the spring, skipping school to wade in the Cautín River with his friends. Innocent pastimes, daydreams, and random reading fed the visions of the poems that he was already writing on scraps of paper that he kept hidden from his father.

During vacations the Reyes family went to a nearby beach called Baja Imperial that later appears in the famous poem "A Song of Despair" in the volume that catapulted Neruda to fame at an early age: *Veinte poemas de amor y una canción desesperada (Twenty Love Poems and a Song of Despair)*. Rain, sea, forest, and sawmills populate the poetic and imaginary world of the young Neftalí.

But he outgrew the provincial life and after finishing his secondary studies, in March 1921, went to live in the capital. Neruda, taking only a few possessions, boarded a third-class train for Santiago. He immortalized the trip to Santiago in one of his poems, "El tren nocturno" ("The Night Train"):

> Oh largo tren nocturno,
> muchas veces
> desde el sur hacia el norte,
> entre ponchos mojados
>
> (The long night train,
> so often
> south to north,
> with wet ponchos)
>
> (p. 60)

Even before Neftalí Reyes arrived in Santiago he had made a name for himself in the small literary circles of the province. In 1919 he won the prize for the city of Temuco in the competition "Los juegos florales," a national poetry competition celebrated each spring throughout Chile. It was then that he adopted the pseudonym with which he became world famous: Pablo Neruda—Neruda after a nineteenth-century Czech author named Ian Neruda (1834–91), a leader of the Eastern European symbolist school. Ian Neruda was a short story writer and journalist and one of the most beloved poets of Czechoslovakia. The Chilean's choice of his first name is a mystery, but in Hebrew "Paul" means "he who says beautiful things."

He was tall, extremely thin, and impoverished as well. He wore a great cape inherited from his father and a brimmed hat that would become famous in his walks around the capital, where he was the very image of the pale, romantic poet. Five years later, Neruda's followers, when reading his poetry, would copy his dress as well as his nasal, melancholy voice. By now Neruda was known in the literary circles of the capital, and, in 1921, while studying to be a French teacher at the University of Chile, he was awarded the first prize of the Student Federation for his poem "Canción de la fiesta" (Fiesta song), which was printed in a beautiful edition by the publishing house of the Federation itself. Neruda was writing for the student newspaper, *Claridad,* and until 1926 for several other journals. He also founded and edited the journal *Caballo de Bastos.* He translated some of Rilke's *Notebooks of Malte Laurid Brigge,* which resemble Neruda's own *Memoirs (Confieso que he vivido),* especially its division into "notebooks."

"Maruri 513" was his first address in Santiago. He says in his memoirs that he spent many hours contemplating the dramatic sunsets from his window. The suggestive title of his book *Crepuscalario,* published and financed by the author himself, evokes those afternoons full of romantic longing, desolation, and bohemian life.

Twenty Love Poems and a Song of Despair came at a time of renovation and change in the world literary scene. In Chile, the poet Vicente Huidobro, like the European avant-garde, was founding the *creacionismo* (creationism) movement whose primordial function was to invent realities that were strictly poetic. This movement and others like it would liberate the poet from his traditional role of simple imitator or reflector of the physical and visible world. The famous phrase of Huidobro in his *Ars poética* reflects this concept: "Oh Poets, why sing of roses? / Let them flower in your poems" (¿Por qué cantáis la rosa, o poetas? / Hazla florecer en el poema).[4]

The year 1924 marks a watershed in the poetic route of Neruda. In that year, he published *Twenty Love Poems and a Song of Despair.* The unexpected impact of this slim volume of poetry on Spanish-American and world poetry cannot be overemphasized. In it, an adolescent speaks to a woman of sensual and erotic love with a clarity and simplicity of expression unknown until then in Spanish-language poetry.

During this time Neruda also came under the influence of the latest currents of European literary movements, especially French surrealism. In 1924 André Bréton, in Paris, published the *First Surrealist Manifesto,*[5] proclaiming the expression of the artistic impulse through the subconscious. In this *Manifesto,* Bréton explains that the way to a superreality could be found by liberating the mind of logical and rational coordinates. This technique would be a productive one for Neruda in his collection entitled *Residencia en la tierra (Residence on Earth).*

In 1926 Neruda published three books that fit into the avant-garde movement: *Tentativa del hombre infinito* (Venture of the infinite man), *Anillos* (Rings), and the brief poetic novel, *El habitante y su esperanza* (The inhabitant and his hope), all of which will be treated in chapter 3.

At the age of twenty-three Neruda was a poet whose verses were recited, read, and celebrated by a wide Spanish-American public, especially the young. But just as the city of Temuco and its forests became an all too familiar territory for him, so too did the capital. Neruda decided to travel and to explore new lands. He was appointed consul of Chile to Burma, and in 1927 he arrived in Rangoon to assume his post. He stayed until 1929, when he was sent to Colombo (Ceylon), Batavia (Java), and Singapore.

While for other Latin American poets such as Octavio Paz, the Orient was a site of reconciliation and encounter with the interior equilibrium represented by Oriental philosophies, for Neruda, the opposite phenomenon occurred. The Far East became for him a place of alienation and solitude. A spiritual malaise took hold of his being, and his poetry changed radically. His language, previously characterized by its sculpted precision and graphic clarity, became hermetic, in order to transmit his visceral intuition of a disintegrating world that he was doomed to traverse alone. The language and style of this new phase gives birth to the book *Residence on Earth,* which represents one of the poetic landmarks of Spanish-American letters.

The year 1930 was an important one for Neruda. He was married to Maria Antonieta Hagenaar, an Indonesian woman of Dutch extraction. Of this union was born, on 6 December 1934, the poet's only child, Malva Marina. Little has been written about this marriage or about Neruda as a father. We know only that Malva Marina died in 1942.

The Spanish Years

With his mission in the East ended, Neruda moved with his wife and child to Spain, first to Barcelona, where he was to serve as consul of Chile, and the next year to Madrid. The period in Spain was quite different from his alienating experience in the Orient. In Madrid Neruda came into immediate contact with the Spanish poets, especially García Lorca, whom he had met earlier in Buenos Aires, Rafael Alberti, Manuel Altolaguirre, and Miguel Hernández. This community of poets and Neruda's influence on Peninsular poetry bring to mind the triumph in the mother country of another Spanish American, Rubén Darío, the founder of Hispanic modernism. Darío, twenty years before, played a role of great importance in the poetic community, as did Neruda. Darío too had published his first important book of poetry, *Azul* (Blue) (1888), in Chile and then gone to Spain, where he became a poetic harbinger of Spanish America.

This poetic fraternity was torn apart by the outbreak of the Spanish Civil War in 1936. As Neruda watched the Falangists destroy his house and the contents of his journal *Caballo Verde para la Poesia* (Green horse for poetry), he was filled with pain and foreboding. His consular assignment was taken away from him, and shortly after the beginning of the war his wife left him and returned to the Netherlands.

In 1934 Neruda met the Argentinian painter Delia del Carril, affectionately called by her friends *la hormiguita,* the "little ant," because of her untiring work in a myriad of causes from politics to poetry. Pablo Neruda and Delia, who still lives in a huge house filled with her own paintings on Lynch Street in Santiago, were together for over twenty years. This strong and inspiring woman remained beside him during politically difficult times: the Spanish Civil War, part of the Second World War in Europe, and the period of persecutions against him by the González Videla regime in Chile.

In 1936 Neruda's close friend García Lorca was killed by the Falangists in Granada. Neruda, before leaving Spain in February 1937, went to Paris to deliver a moving tribute to his friend Lorca, whose name appears continually in his books and especially in his *Memoirs.*

The Spanish period marks the formation of Neruda's political and social conscience. Among his activities was assisting Spanish exiles to obtain passage to Latin America. Before his return to Chile he attended an important writers' conference in Paris. Also present were Alexei Tolstoy of the Soviet Union, Tristan Tzara and Julien Benda of France, Vicente Huidobro of Chile, and from Peru that other great poet of Spanish America, César Vallejo, with whom Neruda would found the organization Spanish American Aid to

Spain. All these political activities, especially at the International Writers' Conference, mark the end of his hermetic isolation. He became powerfully dedicated to political action and would remain so throughout the rest of his life.

When he returned to Santiago, Neruda founded an organization called the Intellectual Alliance of Chile. That same year in Chile, he published in four consecutive editions *España en el corazón (Spain in My Heart)*, where the bitter experience of the Spanish Civil War was chronicled. The Spanish poet Manuel Altolaguirre had edited that volume on the battlefront during the battle of Barcelona and even manufactured the paper for it to be printed on. This book was incorporated into *Tercera residencia (Third Residence)* (1935–45), published in a 1947 Buenos Aires edition that included the long poem *Las furias y las penas (The Furies and the Sorrows)* and *Spain in My Heart*.

The hermetic nature of the earlier *Residences* was replaced by a documentary chronicle style with a historical and epic tone. This reorientation brought about by the Spanish Civil War has particular importance for Neruda as a poet and as a man. He is now increasingly drawn to a tradition that proclaims a shared ideology. It was the Spanish experience that brought about a new philosophy that we will see in another of his great volumes of poetry: *Canto general* (General song) (1950) where Neruda, inspired by Spain, turns to American themes. We might mention, too, that another great South American poet, the Peruvian César Vallejo, dedicated a poem to the mother country, in his collection "España, aparta de mí este cáliz" (Spain, take this cup from me) (1937–38).

From Spain to America

During the decade of 1940–50, Neruda's travels were limited to Spanish America with the exception of his first trip to the Soviet Union in 1949. He went to Mexico City as consul in 1941. The year 1942 found him in Guatemala and Cuba where he became acquainted with a totally different landscape and history. In 1943, another pilgrimage took him to the Inca city of Macchu Picchu (also called Machu Picchu), which inspired him to write his spectacular poem, *The Heights of Macchu Picchu*, the key poem of *Canto general*.

On his return to Chile in 1945 Neruda was elected Communist party senator from the northern mining provinces. He also received

a major honor from his country: the National Prize of Literature.
But along with these triumphs, there is another side. González
Videla, running for president on a nationalist platform, asked Neruda for political support, which Neruda generously gave. But once
elected, González Videla betrayed his political platform and became
little more than a tool of foreign investment interests. In 1947
Neruda, then in Caracas, wrote a powerful document attacking
Videla. It was called "Carta íntima para millones de hombres" (An
intimate letter to millions of men) and ultimately resulted in his
suspension from his post as senator.[6] The next year, the Chilean
government ordered his arrest, the Communist party was dissolved,
and its members obliged to go underground. Neruda went from
home to home, seeking refuge, and was sheltered by families of all
social classes.

He continued writing poems, clandestinely, poems that reflect
rage and pain at his persecution. They are testimonies of great lyrical
force and political sentiment. In 1949 he crossed the Andes on
horseback toward a painful exile that was to have profound implications for his poetry. Upon receiving the Nobel Prize in 1971 he
remembered the experience in the Andes:

No había huellas, no existían senderos y con mis cuatro compañeros a
caballo buscábamos en ondulante cabalgata- eliminando los obstáculos de
poderosos árboles, imposibles ríos, roqueríos inmensos, desoladas nieves,
adivinando más bien- el derrotero de mi propia libertad.

(There were no tracks and no paths, and I and my four companions, riding
on horseback, pressed forward on our tortuous way, avoiding the obstacles
set by huge trees, impossible rivers, immense cliffs and desolate expanses
of snow, blindly seeking the quarter in which my own liberty lay.)[7]

From this journey through mountain passes come the first poetic
inspirations that will make for a reencounter with the New World:
America.

During a trip to Mexico, Neruda met Matilde Urrutia, whom he
had seen briefly in 1946 at an open air concert in Santiago. This
woman, who inspired much of his love poetry, would be his companion until his death in 1973. Matilde's presence, inseparable
thereafter from his poetry, transformed Neruda's abstract vision into
a more concrete, earthbound one. Matilde inspired a reorientation
of Neruda's life. Between 1949 and 1956 Matilde and Neruda

carried on a discreet liaison. From 1952 all the poet's books bespeak her presence, evident especially in *Los versos del capitan* (*The Captain's Verses*) and *Cien sonetos del amor* (*One Hundred Love Sonnets*), as well as in fragments of *Barcarola* (*Barcarole*). Thus we see that this love is closely linked to the presence of amorous lyricism.

In Mexico, Neruda published *Canto general* with illustrations by the famous muralists Diego Rivera and David Alfaro Siqueiros. This book, which in Chile could be sold only clandestinely, circulated freely in such countries as Poland, Czechoslovakia, and the Soviet Union. The year 1950 is a triumphant one for Neruda and a period during which the poet travels throughout the American continent, Europe, and even India, where he is granted an audience with Nehru. In the same year he attends the World Conference for Peace in Warsaw, where he receives, together with Pablo Picasso, the International Prize for Peace for his poem "Que despierte el leñador" (Let the wood cutter awake) of *Canto general*. The adage "No one is a prophet in his own land" applies well to Neruda in this period. In spite of his triumphs abroad, he, like many Latin American writers, was forced to live in exile because of his political beliefs.

In 1952 he published anonymously *The Captain's Verses* in the romantic Island of Capri, a collection of love poetry inspired by Matilde. Neruda later confessed that the anonymity was meant to protect the feelings of Delia del Carril, to whom he was still legally married.

In Isla Negra

When the Chilean government declared an amnesty for Neruda in 1950, the poet returned to his country, which he had never truly abandoned, for Chile appears in all or most of his many books. He returns to Temuco, that land moistened by the constant rains. He travels throughout the country as if returning to rediscover the roots of childhood—the ocean and the aroma of wood.

After this return to the springs of his existence, Neruda began moving toward a transparent form of poetic expression. The grandiloquence of the *Canto general* vanished, and he began to speak of all manner of material objects, giving them nobility and a life of their own. He wrote odes to onions, to coffee cups, to the dictionary, and even to the Chilean national dish, *congrio frito*, fried eel. In the *Odas* (*Odes*) the objects of daily life always appear in the foreground.

From the collective experience of a continent, represented in the *Canto general,* Neruda turns his gaze towards the simple objects that serve human needs.

At fifty-two years of age, Pablo Neruda was awarded the first Stalin Prize for Peace, and his poetic activity continued to be exuberant. In 1956 Losada published his complete works in Buenos Aires, and by now most of the books by Neruda had been translated into almost all the languages of the globe.

With the earnings from his books, Neruda built several houses, one in Valparaíso, called La Sebastiana after the builder and architect, Sebastián Coyado. The best-loved home of all, his house in Isla Negra, was bought in 1939 and later renovated. The fabled Isla Negra is neither "island" nor "black." It is simply a fishing village some sixty kilometers from Santiago. The house was designed by Neruda to be all stone, and it has marvelous objects collected from his trips around the world, for example, outside enormous figureheads, and, inside, shells, bottles, rare books, and in the garden, an immense bell that whistles with the wind and sea of Isla Negra. In *Una casa en la arena* (A house on the sand) (1966) Neruda, in poetic prose, sings to this place where he composed the verses that defined these lands and taught the rest of the world something about them. He says in his *Memoirs:*

En mi casa he reunido juguetes pequeños y grandes, sin los cuales no podría vivir. He edifidcado mi casa también como un juguete y juego en ella de la mañana a la noche.

(In my house I have put together a collection of small and large toys I can't live without. I have also built my house like a toy house and I play in it from morning 'til night.) (*Memoirs,* p. 268)

In 1970 Neruda was found to be ill with cancer. Nonetheless the next year he was named ambassador to France and received the Nobel Prize for literature. In his acceptance speech he again spoke of the place on earth that signified so much for him—southern Chile, with its great forests, ever-mysterious backlands, and cool rivers that bathe the skin. Above all, he reiterated a continued belief in poetry as communication with oneself and with others. Salvador Allende, elected to the presidency of Chile in that year, gave a speech at the National Stadium in Santiago to celebrate publicly Neruda's Nobel award.

In 1972 Neruda returned to Chile, to Isla Negra, to his home, with all its beloved objects, near the Pacific. He tells us in his *Memoirs* of the jubilant crowd that awaited him in the National Stadium on his return. But the conditions in Chile were steadily worsening, as was the poet's own. Margarita Aguirre, the poet's niece, in her extensive and detailed *Las vidas de Pablo Neruda,* tells us that he was weary, suffering from rheumatism and cancer, and remained isolated from public life. But his ardent support for his friend Salvador Allende continued. His political book, *Incitación al Nixoncidio y alabanza de la revolución chilena (A Call for the Destruction of Nixon and Praise for the Chilean Revolution,* 1973), was published by Quimantú, a Chilean publishing house founded by Salvador Allende so that books could be made accessible to all. This book of Neruda's, as well as several successive books of poetry, was written in the readily recognizable green ink he always used when writing.

Though bedridden, Neruda continued writing his memoirs and, with Matilde at his side, was looking forward to his seventieth birthday. Neruda always enjoyed celebrations with the almost child-like optimism so characteristic of him. But the advancing cancer prevented him from ever reaching that twelfth of July 1974. At the same time that a military coup d'état was staged, Neruda's health suddenly worsened. With troops blocking the streets, an ambulance that had been called for him was not permitted to pass. He died at his home on 23 September 1973. The death of Pablo Neruda, who vindicated Latin American poetry in the eyes of the world and especially in his own country, coincides with the death of another person, Salvador Allende, who symbolizes the Latin American democratic spirit. With their passing ends a period of hope lived by the Chilean people.

Neruda's funeral was an important event for the Chilean and Spanish-American people. A multitude accompanied him to the general cemetery, singing the national anthem of Chile and the International, as he surely would have wished. It was a brave demonstration of the Chilean people who, despite the repressive measures imposed by the coup, took to the streets for the man who had sung for them and their land. Matilde Urrutia has requested reburial in Isla Negra, but at this writing, government permission has still not been granted. It is fitting that Neruda return to the site at Isla Negra that meant so much to him and someday we hope he will.

Meanwhile Chileans continue to visit his grave on his birthdate and to view his house on the shore.

At the time Neruda was dying, his beloved Chile was a divided country. Augusto Pinochet and the armed forces attacked the Presidential Palace where, inside, President Salvador Allende, met his death. Neruda's homes in Santiago and Valparaíso were vandalized and the workers for whom Neruda recited his verses were hunted down, and many were imprisoned or killed. The Chilean singer and guitarist Víctor Jara who set to music the famous "Poema XV" from *Twenty Love Poems,* died in the National Stadium, where thousands of prisoners were held, with his hands both physically and symbolically mutilated.

Neruda's poetry remains to remind us that neither the man nor his creations truly vanish. His life takes the form of a kaleidoscope revolving about a constant center, as we have seen with the landscape of Temuco that is always with him. In that center is an image of rain, rivers, and freight trains that connote a wider American reality. The substance of his poetry is terrestrial, material, and telluric. Neruda's poetry is joined to the social and political future of the American continent.

Neruda maintains tenaciously his role of poet and does not theorize or double as critic. He is a keeper of his intimacy—he believes that one learns poetry at its primal sources, like an artisan "of bread, truth, wine, dreams."[8]

Chapter Two
Love Poetry

Twenty Love Poems and a Song of Despair

Neruda has long been considered a poet of love who constantly describes the sentiments that accompany sensuality and eroticism. Indeed, a glance at his extensive poetic production shows the theme of love to be pervasive. In this chapter we shall study those books that manifest the development of this dimension: *Twenty Love Poems and a Song of Despair, The Captain's Verses, One Hundred Love Sonnets,* and part of *Barcarole.* The evolution of the love theme is inseparable from Neruda's own poetic voyage.

Neruda's first book, *Crepusculario,* of 1923 follows the patterns set by Chilean romantic poetry of the last century, mixed with traces of modernism—that Spanish-American literary current that swept the continent from 1888 to 1916 and that was the first original literary movement originating in Spanish America. *Crepusculario* consists of regular rhymed and measured verses in traditional meter, especially the Alexandrine. Later, in *Twenty Love Poems,* Neruda abandons traditional metrics for blank verse in an effort to find his own style, distinct from that of his predecessors.

Romantic motifs such as melancholy and the exotic predominate in *Crepusculario.* We see Neruda's familiarity with Maeterlinck, especially *Pelleas and Melisandra,* and detect other influences from French romantic poetry as well. *Crepusculario,* however, with its hints of passion, also foreshadows the eroticism of the *Twenty Love Poems* where love is a route to liberation and an escape from solitude.

In *Crepusculario* Neruda dwells on the idea of love as absence and loneliness. He uses a simile well known to Chilean youth, where love is the sailor who reaches port for a brief stay, only to depart once more. We shall see this simile of love as fleeting happiness followed by abandonment echoing throughout his work.

Crepusculario, a brief book that had been rejected by Nascimento, the most prestigious publishing house in Chile at the time, was published nonetheless with the help of the most distinguished literary figure of the period, the critic Hernán Díaz Arrieta. Also known by his pen name "Alone," Díaz Arrieta had served as mentor to such writers as Gabriela Mistral, Marta Brunet, Pedro Prado, and Eduardo Barrios.

The *Twenty Love Poems* appears at a fortuitous moment, at a time when in Europe as in Latin America, the search for a new language and expression dominates the spirit of the age. Neruda played a key role in this movement for renovation, in which Spanish-American poetry began to relinquish its traditional forms and enter the modern age. This book also marks a clear transition from the era of Spanish-American modernism to that of surrealism, with its often disconnected images and metaphors, which will dominate Neruda's next phase. Neruda's simplicity, sparse imagery, and above all, unabashed expression of amorous sentiments were innovations that immediately commanded the attention of the reading public.

Without revolutionizing language completely or giving himself over excessively to avant-garde trends such as the automatic writing of some surrealists, Neruda found a golden mean for his poetry in the balance between a subjective conception and a constriction of imagery. As the critic Hernán Loyola suggests, these poems relate a nebulous story of love, from the first infatuation to the explosion of passion and, finally, in the "Desperate Song," the parting of the lovers.[1]

The book is brief since brevity is a requisite for maintaining tension. The poetic self is well defined throughout the search for the beloved that begins in the first poem:

> Fui solo como un túnel. De mí huían los pájaros,
> y en mí la noche entraba su invasión poderosa.
> Para sobrevivirme te forjé como un arma,
> como una flecha en mi arco, como una piedra en mi honda.
>
> (I was alone, like a tunnel. The birds fled from me,
> and night swamped me with its crushing invasion.
> To survive myself I forged you like a weapon,
> like an arrow in my bow, a stone in my sling.)[2]

The poem expresses a desire for a union synonymous with an act of survival through woman. This longing for oneness reappears continuously through poem 20, the poem that marks the beginning of the shipwreck image and the tragic separation of the couple. All the previous poems are set in different geographical locations amid summer storms and winds in a lyrical space imbued with the southern landscape and hints of nearby city sounds.

The body of the beloved becomes a landscape in itself, "En tí la tierra canta" ("In you the earth sings") (poem 3) and in poem 10 the beloved leans towards the sunset and is fused with the landscape. Land, twilight, and sunset come together in the *Twenty Love Poems* to create the presence of a magnetic earth with the beloved inscribed within it. In the background is the lyrical voice speaking of solitude, sadness, and loneliness while looking for the other, the "you," a woman of "white thighs," "gray beret," and "oceanic eyes" who always evades him.

Dialogue does not exist, for this is a collection of monologues where desperation, alienation, and the obsessive need to obliterate loneliness constantly seep through. Solipsism is avoided by images that refer to a shared past. The poetic language is enhanced by long rhythmic lines and by a tone of melancholic sobriety, especially at the end.

The image of the woman takes on a transcendental importance in this book, for she is associated with the elements and the earth. She is the earth mother, a notion established by the romantic poets of the last century, but which Neruda makes more immediate and secular: "Te pareces al mundo en tu actitud de entrega" ("You look like a world, lying in surrender") ("Cuerpo de mujer" ["Body of a Woman,"] p. 8).

A marked sensuality appears in each verse, as the female body is associated with a topography of "white hills" and "smiling water" ("Body of a Woman," p. 8). Woman, who plays with the world and resembles that world elevated to a cosmic level, is cast in images of the surrounding natural landscape—sky, water, earth.

The beloved is always united with a sensuous and colorful background landscape. But just as nature is part of woman, her moods, and her body, nature itself vibrates and is humanized in her. The mist and the rivers dance, the waist of the beloved is a waist of mist and her pubis is covered with roses. Again, woman is nature. She is a pine forest, her body is a sprig of wheat, its surface like a map covered by earthly and cosmic elements united in a vast lyrical continuity throughout the book. It is a book celebrating the unforgettable sentiment of first love, which examines afresh the first stirrings of happiness and lucklessness. Even after the shipwreck,

the amorous sentiment survives through the power of language that
is integrated with nature.

Marisol and Marisombra

There is general agreement, based on the recently published love
letters of Neruda, that the *Twenty Love Poems* are implicitly addressed
to two different women, corresponding to the dual poetic structure
of the book. Neruda himself admitted in his *Memoirs* to two love
stories in *Twenty Love Poems:* Marisol, from the two words for "sea"
and "sun," referring to a teen-age love in the south of Chile and
Marisombra, "sea" and "shadow," a love in Santiago. The latter is
represented by a gray beret, sunset reflections, and the desolation
of a large city. The poem with which the book concludes, "Una
canción desesperada" ("The Song of Despair") is dedicated to this
same Marisombra on the occasion of their farewell:

> Todo te lo tragaste, como la lejanía,
> Como el mar, como el tiempo. Todo en tí fue
> naufragío!
>
> (You swallowed everything, like distance,
> Like the sea, like time. In you everything sank!)
> ("The Song of Despair," p. 61)

Despite the biographical distinctions, the two women Marisol-
Marisombra merge into a single voice constructed around the love
object. The suggestive images and similes used to describe these
muses have a material sense, as in "tu cintura de niebla," ("your
waist of mist") or the idea of the embrace that overwhelms: "apegada
a mis brazos como una enredadera" ("clasping my arms like a climb-
ing plant") ("Te recuerdo como eras," "I Remember You as You
Were," p. 20).

These biographical details serve to verify certain tonalities in the
poems. Besides the monothematic lyrical self, there is another aspect
pointed out by Manuel Durán, who in *Earth Tones,* indicates that
Twenty Love Poems forms a chiaroscuro. Light evokes the childhood
of the poet while dark colors evoke his residence in Santiago and
the life of the starving student watching the sunsets from the Maruri
Street pension. Though the identity of the persons for whom the

poems were written is not of textual importance, the existence of two possible loves illuminate our reading of the book.

One of the reasons that *Twenty Love Poems* draws the reader so powerfully is the sobriety of expression and the economy of the images: "Ya no la quiero, es cierto, pero cuánto la quise" ("I no longer love her, that is certain, but how I loved her") ("Tonight I Can Write," p. 57).

Simple, direct words, but within this clarity Neruda leaves open the possibility of an intuitive cognition. For example, in poem 13: "Entre los labios y la voz, algo se va muriendo" ("Between the lips and the voice, something goes dying") ("I Have Gone Marking," p. 39). That poetical suggestion, that "something" that the reader must imagine, constitutes another of the many attractions of the book.

Everyday images take on a poetic force when the lyrical dimension envelops common objects, a technique that the poet will master gradually until it culminates in the book of *Odes* that we will examine later on.

Some examples of this phenomenon can be seen in images such as the sky that is compared to a "net filled with shadowy birds." The sky image is linked to the idea of water through the "nets." Contradictory phrases are used together with similes linked to a series of imaginative associations such as:

> Te recuerdo como eras en el último otoño.
> Eras la boina gris y el corazón en calma.
>
> (I remember how you were in the last autumn.
> You were the gray beret and the still heart.)
> ("I Remember You As You Were," p. 20)

The woman is remembered through the artifice of the beret, whose color evokes autumn. After this free association the poet continues with ordered poetic discourse: "The leaves fell in the water of your soul." Autumn, falling leaves, and the eyes of the beloved are united in a coherent combination born from the initial vision of a woman with a gray beret.

Most of the poems in this book derive from a central governing image such as the body of the beloved, or the memory of a woman in autumn. Poet 6 ("I Remember You as You Were") illustrates how the symmetry of such images clusters throughout. In the second stanza the beloved is compared to a vine, an image that conjures up the idea of a leafy garden and above all, the idea of the beloved's embrace:

> Apegada a mis brazos como una enredadera,
> las hojas recogían tu voz lenta y en calma.
> Hoguera de estupor en que mi ser ardía.
> Dulce jacinto azul torcido sobre mi alma.
>
> (Clasping my arms like a climbing plant,
> the leaves garnered your voice, that was slow and at
>   peace.
> Bonfire of awe in which my thirst was burning.
> Sweet blue hyacinth twisted over my soul.)
>   ("I Remember You As You Were," p. 21)

The themes of distance and absence will be the central focus of the second part of the poem, in direct counterpoint to the first. The motif of memory with which the poem opens culminates with the idea of transience: "Siento viajar tus ojos y es distante el otoño" ("I feel your eyes traveling and the autumn is far off") ("I Remember You As You Were," p. 20). The words "light" and "still pond" are associated directly with the transparency and clarity of the very memory that is being evoked and with the woman's eyes:

> Cielo desde un navío. Campo desde los cerros:
> Tu recuerdo es de luz, de humo, de estanque en
>   calma!
> Más allá de tus ojos ardían los crepúsculos.
> Hojas secas de otoño giraban en tu alma.
>
> (Sky from a ship. Field from the hills:
> Your memory is made of light, of smoke, of a still
>   pond!
> Beyond your eyes, farther on, the evenings were
>   blazing.
> Dry autumn leaves revolved in your soul.)
>   ("I Remember You As You Were," p. 20)

The constant repetition of the verb "era" ("was") emphasizes the sense of aloneness in the poem, while the irregular meter and colloquial syntax also allow the reader to assimilate the experience of absence and parting. The poem concludes with a re-evocation of the autumn and its dessication: "hojas secas de otoño giraban en tu alma" ("dry autumn leaves revolved in your soul"). Each metaphor in the poem is synchronized in symmetry, to create an associated resonance in the mind of the reader.

With more than two million copies printed, *Twenty Love Poems* became one of the most successful books of poetry in the Hispanic world. The force and the freshness of its poems come from an internal coherence beginning with the possession of the beloved object and ending with the loneliness of shipwreck. The emotions of possession and loss are felt gradually as we follow an itinerary of a love that is disintegrating: "Es tan corto el amor y tan largo el olvido" ("Love is so short, and forgetfulness so long") ("Tonight I Can Write," p. 58). The "desperate song" at the end is the manifestation and summation of these sentiments of pain and solitude. This book, after so many years, still delights the reader by its lyrical evocations and transparencies, in its search for woman as a refuge from solitude.

Among the many reiterated images of the *Twenty Love Poems,* the sea is the most constant presence. Poem 18, for example, reinvokes the image of the poet as mariner:

> Este es un puerto.
> Aquí te amo.
>
> (This is a port.
> Here I love you.)
> ("Here I Love You," p. 52)

In poem 17, the sea appears as a confine full of cold objects and old anchors, the same scene that will spill over into the shipwreck in poem 20 and the "desperate song." Thus the sea is constantly joined to the breakup of the lovers.

"The Song of Despair" brings together a group of images associated with the sea, but especially with the absolute abandonment symbolized by shipwreck: "Sobre mi corazón llueven frías corolas" ("Cold flower heads are raining over my heart") ("The Song of Despair," p. 60). Suddenly woman herself is a destructive force: communion with the loved one is not possible. This theme is repeated with desolating force in the book of the *Residences,* especially

in *The Furies and the Sorrows* written in 1936 but published in the
1950s.

For Neruda, fulfilled love will be possible only as a concomitant
of social solidarity *(The Captain's Verses)* or in the encounter with a
unique beloved woman who is simultaneously all women (the *One
Hundred Love Sonnets* written for Matilde Urrutia).

Woman as an essential element of nature and as an integral part
of the cosmos is one of the recurrent ideas in the *Twenty Love Poems.*
We must also mention the sexuality of these poems, where the man
acts as the dominant being who seeks union with the woman.

John Felstiner, in his article "A Feminist Reading of Pablo Neruda" is one of the few critics who mentions the dialectics between
the sexes.[4] Let us look at the key verses that reveal this concept:
"Mi cuerpo de labriego salvaje te socava" ("My rough peasant's body
digs into you") ("Body of a Woman," p. 8). The speaker is seen as
primitive man, whose impulse is to take and possess while the
beloved becomes a physical entity associated with the earth. Again,
the idea of possession is found in this poem: "Para sobrevivir te
forjé como un arma" ("To survive myself, I made you, like a weapon")
("Body of a Woman," p. 8). We find it in the image of a warrior
who takes the woman in erotic ecstasy and shields himself with her.
It also reinforces the central idea of the poet's identity as derived
from the primal act of physical union, for to "survive" his past self,
he must join it to the body of a woman.

Eroticism as a form of cognition and discovery of the other is
implicit in all of *Twenty Love Poems.* It is worth noting that these
forceful and sensual descriptions do not appear in the nostalgic
Crepusculario or in any other of Neruda's poems at this time. The
masculine lyrical speaker who discovers himself through the woman,
who always appears distant, frightened, and silent, reflects the sexual
dialectics of power. She takes the form of a slave, mute and sub-
missive, in contrast to the poet who appears in various poetic
personae: peasant, archer, fisherman, and, of course, the poet creating the text for his audience. This evocation of the beloved implies
that the poet finds in her the direct expression of telluric and cosmic
elements. The woman is the very representation of carnal desire and
lyricism and the source of fulfillment for the male. The frank treat-
ment of the erotic theme undoubtedly explains part of the popularity
the book enjoyed when it was first published. The sensuality with
which the female is described was both arresting and original. The

description of the mons veneris as a rose, the breasts as white snails, and the hips as fresh islands were all audacious steps in Spanish-American poetry.

The imposing presence of the ocean and the images of river, docks, and seas establish an unchanging frame of reference. Water, associated with the subconscious, is coupled with eroticism. In these poems we find an erotic and sensual symbolism using aquatic images to reinforce the idea of movement and fluidity of the bodies that seek to be united, like nets that "don't retain water" (poem 12). The reference to the port as a space where the poet awaits the woman (poem 13) has rhythmic projections in the other poems and eventually culminates in the destructive catharsis of the shipwreck:

> Ese fue mi destino y en él viajó mi anhelo,
> y en él cayó mi anhelo, todo en tí fue naufragio!

> (This was my destiny and it was the voyage of my longing,
> and in it my longing fell, in you everything sank!)
>   ("The Song of Despair," p. 63)

With this conceptualization of woman, Neruda takes another important step in his poetic development. Woman is the silent companion who listens for the poet's invitation to the social struggle. With her he will leave behind adolescent loves and desires and will enter the amorous relationship as an equal, not only propelled by physical desire but by the wish for equality. *The Captain's Verses* will illustrate that phase of shared love.

The reader cannot forget the emotional tension of Neruda's early love poems that won over a generation of young readers to the appreciation of his poetry and that introduced love as a cosmic and sublime force throughout his work. *Twenty Love Poems* is the foundation for the greatest of Neruda's poetry, in which the telluric and the erotic are integrated and become the repeated pantheistic experience, a dialectic of self-discovery through woman and man.

The Captain's Verses

This collection, though published initially in 1952, in Naples, was not recognized by the author as his own until ten years later. The delay occurred because the book was dedicated to a new love, Matilde Urrutia, and Neruda, so as not to hurt Delia del Carril, his wife of many years, chose to publish the book anonymously.[5] It is the first mature book of amorous poetry written by Neruda.

The book was controversial politically as well as personally because at the same time that Neruda was being praised by some Italian public figures, he received an order of expulsion from Italy as a consequence of his activities in the Communist party. Pressure from Italian writers had the expulsion order revoked.

Erwin Cherio, a distinguished Italian historian, invited Neruda to his home on the island of Capri, where many of the poems in this volume were written. Throughout the poems, many references to the sea location and to the beauty of the island appear:

> Recuerdas cuando,
> en invierno,
> llegamos a la isla?
> El Mar hacia nosotros levantaba
> una copa de frío.

> (Do you remember when,
> in winter,
> we reached the island?
> The sea toasted us with a glass of frost.)[6]

This book is divided into seven units that are the chronicle of a love affair, beginning with the description of the beloved's body. Many poems bear titles like these: "Your feet," "Your hands," "Your laughter." The book follows the daily pleasures and sorrows, and finally, the separation of the lovers. Despite its divisions, the book is a single poem recounting the earthly love shared between a man and a woman:

> Tus rodillas, tus senos,
> tu cintura
> faltan en mí como el hueco
> de una tierra sedienta
> de la que desprendieron
> una forma,
> y juntos
> somos completos como un solo río,
> como una sola arena.

(Your knees, your breasts,
your waist
are missing parts of me like the hollow
of a thirsty earth
from which they broke off
a form,
and together
we are complete like a single river,
like a single grain of sand.)
("El alfarero" ["The Potter"], p. 6)

In *The Captain's Verses*, as in *Twenty Love Poems*, woman is allied to the surrounding landscape, though not as the cosmic earth mother. There are also certain resonances from *Twenty Love Poems*, such as when the loved one scatters strands of her long tresses or when her body is compared to the map of the American continent. In *Twenty Love Poems* she was a map of delight, now she is the symbol of a continent:

Cuando miro la forma
de América, en el mapa,
amor, a ti te veo: . . .

(When I look at the shape
of America, on the map,
my love, it is you I see: . . .)
("Pequeña America" ["Little America"], p. 110)

The first poem of *The Captain's Verses* echoes the first of the *Twenty Love Poems*.

suben tus hombros como dos colinas,
tus pechos se pasean por mi pecho,

(your shoulders rise like two hills,
your breasts wander over my breasts,)
("Amor" ["Love"], p. 2)

The difference is that the simple laborer, who in the *Twenty Love Poems* sought the woman's body, is transformed here into a seeker more tender than erotic: "y me inclino a tu boca para besar la tierra" ("and I lean down to your mouth to kiss the earth") ("Love," p. 2).

The parallel between the beginning verses of the two books points to a change in Neruda's poetic orientation. The desperate adolescent longing for a woman to satisfy physical and emotional desires becomes the mature poet seeking the woman in a symbiotic sense. In previous works such as the *Residences,* the concept of love was linked only to a social struggle, but in this book social struggle and love are intertwined, as we see in poems such as "The Flag" and "The Soldier's Love." This intriguing union constitutes the nucleus of *The Captain's Verses.*

Let us not forget the profound repercussions of the Spanish Civil War on Neruda's world view. In 1950 he published *Canto general,* a book dedicated to the definition and the history of the American continent, in it the poet's idea of love is inseparable from social and political activity.

In *Twenty Love Poems* woman is associated with the cosmos and the earth—she is a goddess playing with the universe. Here that grandiloquent idea becomes more elementary and earth-bound. The poet is now sure of the woman he loves and her reciprocated love:

> Cuando vas por las calles
> nadie te reconoce.
>
> (When you go through the streets
> no one recognizes you.)
>   ("La reina" ["The Queen"], p. 4)[7]

It is implied that only the poet recognizes the anonymous woman, for their bond is strong and permanent.

Several poems exemplify the idea of the woman as companion in a social struggle. For example, the poem "La pobreza" ("Poverty") indicates a rejection of costly garments and riches. The poet speaks to his love, urging her to wear her tattered clothes and shoes without shame. He sees her as a courageous participant in the forces of change who must apply her efforts in unison with men.

The poet no longer tries to transform himself through the application of another's redeeming love but is willing to be a guide who accepts the beloved as comrade in arms. Love is presented as a given, as a stable relationship that will not be severed as in *Twenty Love Poems* but continues as an established configuration. In "La bandera" ("The Flag") there is also an interesting affirmation of what the woman should be in contrast to what she was. The lyrical speaker says that she cannot again dance in her silk ballroom gown. In "Soldier's Love" the poet insists that even with torn shoes she will accompany the soldier in his venture. The woman no longer belongs in a bourgeois setting, where she was mere adornment, because now she will grow with the man, and both are soldiers in arms against the injustices of society.

The lovers in *The Captain's Verses* remain united by devotion to a political cause. They clean the rifle, travel, and march united. The outpouring of eroticism is diminished in this collection, which is marked by simplicity of expression and imagery. The lines are short and direct, and the world appears as something tangible with a clear hierarchy of values. The turbulent and somewhat monotonous "I" becomes completely identified with his beloved as well as with other human beings:

> Ay vida mía,
> no sólo el fuego entre nosotros arde
> sino toda la vida,
> la simple historia,
> el simple amor
> de una mujer y un hombre
> parecidos a todos.
>
> (Ah, my life,
> it is not only the fire that burns between us
> but all of life,
> the simple story,
> the simple love
> of a woman and a man
> like everyone.)
> ("No sólo el fuego" ["Not Only the Fire"], p. 103)

Though there is a decided change of direction in the female image from one book to the other, we must also consider that she continues to be the receptacle of the poet's beliefs. Yesterday's search was that of a lonely adolescent who is now in communion with "the other."

An explicit contradiction exists in the collection. On the one hand, the woman occupies a traditional position of servant and camp-follower and on the other hand, she is described as combatant for social justice, participating with the man fearlessly though she is

never his equal. He, the man, appears as the creator and the god.
She is small, fragile, and it is through him she lives.

Although the man's power is immediately established, the woman,
due to her anatomy and her power of procreation, is the earth mother:

> y vuelves a ser contigo
> la tierra que tú eres:
> eres mi profunda primavera:
> vuelvo a saber en ti cómo germino.

> (and with you I become again
> the earth that you are:
> you are deep spring in me:
> in you I know again how I am born.)
>   ("Oda y germinaciones" ["Ode and Burgeonings"],
>   p. 114)

Another revealing poem, set in a seascape, is "La noche en la
isla" ("Night on the Island") where woman is associated with both
the earth and the cosmos. The first verse begins in a narrative mode:

> Toda la noche he dormido contigo
> junto al mar en la isla.
> Salvaje y dulce eras entre el placer y el sueño,
> entre el fuego y el agua.

> (All night I have slept with you
> next to the sea, on the island.
> Wild and sweet you were between pleasure and sleep,
> between fire and water.)
>   ("Night on the Island," p. 25)

The last two verses reflect a parallelism between the two elements,
fire and water on the one hand, and the pleasures of love making
and of sleep, on the other. The fire appears to act as a unifier of
living things, while water complements it as life-giving substance.
With these two elements Neruda creates an image with the lovers
at the center surrounded by the essential forces necessary for the
proliferation of life.

The last stanza of the poem is related to the first through the
repetition of the image of the lovers sleeping together on the island.

The mouth of the beloved, upon waking, is still a projection of
telluric forces and even carries the taste of earth, seasalt, and seaweed:

> He dormido contigo
> y al despertar, tu boca,
> salida de tu sueño,
> me dio el sabor de tierra,
> de agua marina, de algas,
> del fondo de tu vida,
> y recibí tu beso
> mojado por la aurora
> como si me llegara
> del mar que nos rodea.
>
> (I have slept with you
> and on waking, your mouth,
> come from your dream,
> gave me the taste of earth,
> of seawater, of seaweed,
> of the depths of your life,
> and I received your kiss
> moistened by the dawn
> as if it came to me
> from the sea that surrounds us.)
>   ("Night on the Island," p. 25)

The relationship between man and woman is posited as intrinsically united to the superior forces of nature that are a constant
presence in *The Captain's Verses*. It is implied that both the lyrical
speaker and his beloved are immersed in these forces and in their
purifying atmosphere. The island in this poem represents a refuge
against the assault of the sea and the subconscious world. At the
same time the island is the conciliating union of consciousness and
desire, manifested in the bond between two lovers.

Woman represents the path to self-knowledge, an idea found also
in the love poetry of Octavio Paz. The root concept is a rich metaphor
that reappears in all Neruda's subsequent lyrics as an aspiration
towards pantheistic union and longing for unity with nature.

In "Epitalamio" ("Epithalamium") Neruda introduces a new simile in which the beloved is compared to a small leaf from a tree that
takes root in him:

> hasta que tus raíces
> horadaron mi pecho,
> se unieron a los hilos de mi sangre,
> hablaron por mi boca,
> florecieron conmigo.
>
> (until your roots
> pierced my chest,
> joined the threads of my blood,
> spoke through my mouth,
> flourished with me.)
>   ("Epithalamium," p. 130)

The poem "Epithalamium" reveals a great deal about the general thematics of *The Captain's Verses*. The poetic habitat—the island, the night, and the sea—is the constant locus that permeates the collection, just as the concept of woman as a small fragile figure whose image becomes amplified when it is incorporated in the social struggle is found throughout. In this same poem, though there are no ideological allusions, the woman, the small "leaf," takes on primal and mythic characteristics. Her roots fill the chest of her lover, speak through his mouth, and flower. The woman as muse has the same proportions as the mother earth that permits the union of man to his roots. This poem exemplifies the dialectical essence of the woman in *The Captain's Verses*. She is dependent on her lover but is also the reincarnation of the earth itself.

John Felstiner says that the woman "literally comes after her man, completes his being, cleaves to him; that she is of the earth and that only through him is she of the spirit."[7] Woman continues to be the total conjugation of earth, fragrance, primal origin, and destiny, and it is she who restores the poet to concrete reality.

The beloved is often described in affectionate terms of size. In "La infinita" ("The Infinite One") the poet's hands cannot contain or even grasp all the beauty that exists in the woman, "my little tower" the delicate woman who has "firm little feet." Likewise in "Love" the woman is the key to synthesize these diminutive images:

> Pequeña
> Rosa
> rosa pequeña
> a veces,
> diminuta y desnuda

```
                         (Little
                         Rose
                         roselet
                         at times,
                         tiny and nude)
                             ("Love," p. 2)
```

Her figure grows in the presence of her lover because "en el amor como agua de mar te has desatado" ("in love you have loosened yourself like sea water") ("Love," p. 2). Love as a movement of expansion is a basic tendency in *The Captain's Verses* because its redemptive power brings about the union of man and woman, giving meaning to the world and to the details of everyday existence.

The Captain's Verses are written in the context of a hidden passion and also of the political problems that haunt the poet. The small edition of only forty-eight numbered copies printed in Naples is a treasure for all those who identify with these love verses dedicated to a single woman and by extension to all women. Love is the vehicle that gives meaning to the world, for it is desire and also daily reality, a meeting of prosaic and lyrical realities:

```
                    Te veo
                    lavando mis pañuelos,
                    colgando en la ventana
                    mis calcetines rotos . . .

                    (I see you
                    washing my handkerchiefs,
                    hanging at the window
                    my worn out socks)
                        ("Not Only the Fire," p. 102)
```

One Hundred Love Sonnets

The same concept of communion, solidarity, and the love of simple things that emerged in *The Captain's Verses* is continued in these love sonnets dedicated to Matilde Urrutia.[8] In order to understand the lyrical components of these sonnets we must visualize Isla Negra, where they were written and where Neruda spent most of his time after 1960. Isla Negra is a small fishing village some sixty kilometers from the port of Valparaíso. It was in Valparaíso that Rubén Darío, father of Spanish-American modernism, published the book that made him famous, *Azul* (Blue), in 1888.

Isla Negra is a rustic spot of unpaved streets without electricity. The waves break furiously on a beach of hard sand full of agates. The poet's house, with large windows overlooking the Pacific, is best described in his book *Una casa en la arena* (House in the sand), dedicated to the house and its surroundings. The ocean, with its waves and shells, the sound of the wind and the bells, are all elements of the untamed nature that Neruda incorporated into these sonnets as well as into so much of his poetry.

Neruda chooses the traditional Italian sonnet form of fourteen lines but does not follow the rhyme scheme characteristic of the sonnet. The lines are short, and one metaphor is enough to reveal the sentiment: "Ay, amar es un viaje con agua y con estrella" ("Ah, love is a voyage with water and a star") (sonnet 12, *New Decade*, p. 61).

The poet mentions in his prologue that these sonnets are "about wood." Ben Belitt, in a perceptive critique of the sonnets, says the following: "The *Cien sonetos de amor* . . . it accomplishes the miracle of transforming that most servile and feudal of forms—the sonnet's long complaints of knightly self denial and court compliments contrived for the express delectation of a patron—into a husband's book of hours, grievances, privacies, troubled meditations."[9]

The images, now familiar to us from previous Neruda poems, are those of nature reflected in the female body yet tinted with domesticity. In sonnet 12 he surveys the woman's body, navigating its rivers and traversing its villages until its genital fire consumes him in delight.

The idea of navigation and exploring the female body seems to mean for Neruda cognition and creation, with the slumber that follows it representing fulfillment, just as in *The Captain's Verses* there is the idea of shared slumber that translates to communion of the spirit.

The sonnets are divided into four parts: morning, noon, afternoon, and night, which correspond to the seasons in a man's life. The poet and Matilde are the only characters who appear, and Matilde never speaks. The rest of the sonnets are filled with images of the seascapes of Isla Negra: water, salt, sand, birds, and bells. Through Matilde and her serene, mature love, Neruda also returns to the images of his early childhood—the smell of wood and rain, and the roots of a past that is not lost to the lyrical imagination. All these elements come into the poems. Sonnet 5 says:

> Desde Quinchamalí donde hicieron tus ojos
> hasta tus pies creados para mí en la Frontera
> eres la greda oscura que conozco:
> en tus caderas toco de nuevo todo el trigo.

> (From Quinchamalí where they made your eyes,
> to your feet, shaped for me on the frontier
> you are the dark clay:
> in your hips I touch the grain anew.)
> (sonnet 5, Losada ed., p. 15)

In the next sonnet, the poet finds his love in the abandoned roots of the land lost in infancy. In sonnet 29 he returns to the origins of the loved one. Like him, she comes from the south of Chile, whose simplicity and poverty she retains. The sonnet closes with a beautiful image of continuity of the generations:

> Eres del pobre Sur, de donde viene mi alma;
> en su cielo tu madre sigue lavando ropa
> con mi madre. Por eso te escogí, compañera.

> (You come from the destitute South that once nurtured my soul;
> in her heaven, your mother goes on washing clothes
> with my mother. Therefore I have singled you out to be my
>   companion.)
> (sonnet 29, *New Decade,* p. 64)

This loved one is the clay of the earth, with kisses fresh as watermelon. The essentials of life, like bread and wood, are contained in her. She is real because, as the poet says in sonnet 8, she embraces only that which exists: the sand, the tree, and the rain.

Besides the description of the loved one we find the poet singing to the objects he saw around him in his house and on the beach. Nature responds to their love and will grow around them, as we see in sonnet 32 where the two inhabit the house in Isla Negra with no other purpose but to exist in its natural disarray. In sonnet 33 the house is a place designated especially for love, where all nature is integrated and vines climb the steps. The summer, personified, is a nude foot like the foot of the ivy.

The images parallel closely those of *Twenty Love Poems,* where the loved one has almost magical qualities, and the poet crowns her with southern laurels and herbs. Also in sonnet 34 he insists once more on the union of the loved one and of the powerful ocean. She is daughter of the sea and cousin of oregano. In sonnet 36 she is queen of celery, and the poet gives the impression that in her everything lives. This celebration of simple things like oil, wine, and garlic will take on a new vitality and animation in the *Odes,* where they become objects of consumption and delight.

Optimism and vitality are the central characteristics of *One Hundred Love Sonnets.* Even when some poems dedicated to night speak of death, there exists the concept that a strong love will transcend life's end.

Matilde Urrutia is at the center of this kiss, but the possibility of communion through sleep and dreams is also the possibility of resurrection. In sonnet 90 where we find the idea of approaching death, the figure of Matilde appears robed in light, representing redemption from death:

> Hay sólo tu mirada para tanto vacío,
> sólo tu claridad para no seguir siendo,
> sólo tu amor para cerrar la sombra.
>
> (Ay! there is only your face to fill up the vacancy,
> only your clarity pressing back on the whole of nonbeing,
> only your love, where the dark of the world closes in.)
> (sonnet 90, *New Decade,* p. 80)

Neruda's love poetry is vast and appears in one form or another throughout his lyrical production. Even in the *Residences* there are poems like the famous "Widow's Tango" dedicated to a Burmese woman, Josie Bliss. In *Canto general* (1950) the physical description of the poet's mother resembles that of Matilde in the *One Hundred Love Sonnets* with its associated images of plants and earth. But in the fundamental books of love poetry we have studied here, there is a clear trajectory consistent with the concept of woman as part of the earth and the search for her as a way of returning to primal earth and ancestral roots. This journey is initiated in the *Twenty*

Love Poems and completed in Neruda's maturity, in the *One Hundred Love Sonnets*.

On the path that leads from *Crepusculario,* lightly tinged with modernism, through the languid romanticism of *Twenty Love Poems,* the poet's longing for possession of the beloved object subsides only to gain a new vitality in his mature work. Now, after *Canto general,* where love is not addressed to one woman but to a whole continent, he can return to an intimate tone that describes a new vision of love. In simple verses, his images fluctuate between the daily and the mystical, always exuding optimism and confidence. The differences among the books are notable, but even more striking are the similarities. Nature as the source and secret of eroticism is the thread that binds together Neruda's love poetry.

The same tonalities used in *Twenty Love Poems* are echoed here in *One Hundred Love Sonnets.* Colors are used with great effectiveness to represent Matilde wandering in a rainbow of yellows, ambers, and browns of wheat, clay, and autumn. The sonnets are painted in the luminosity of morning and noon as well as in the shadows of nightfall and evening. In the section for "morning" the images allude to earth and clay. The hues darken and the images take on increasing tension as they foretell an ending. The poet does not envision himself dying alone, but with Matilde, her heart tied to his own.

One Hundred Love Sonnets represents the culmination of Neruda's love poetry in the sense that the figure of Matilde subsumes all previous female models, she is the concrete and yet mystical: "Plena mujer, manzana carnal, luna caliente" ("Carnal apple, woman incarnate, incandescent moon") (sonnet 12, *New Decade,* p. 208). She has all the qualities that from time immemorial are associated with the woman, like the moon. The sensuality of the beloved is not only that of Matilde Urrutia, it also has full transcendence and power as cosmic regenerator. These sonnets bring together eroticism, intensity of love, and concrete desire.

Through these texts we see more than ever that the woman, in the amorous poetry of Neruda, is a natural and centrifugal force uniting man with the earth. The images that appear over and over in the love poetry of Neruda, images such as water, humid forests, and the female body likened to American topography are among the most enduring and most significant aspects of Neruda's work. Despite many transformations the lyrical voice of the love poetry is fundamentally the same: rich in sensuality and corporality. An entire

generation was awakened to poetry by these love poems that culminate in the maturity of *One Hundred Love Sonnets*.

Barcarola

It is important that in discussing the theme of love in Neruda's
work that we mention the *Barcarola (Barcarole)*, a long, narrative
poem published in 1967 and often neglected by literary critics.[10]
In it we find the union of the popular and the lyrical that has ever
been a source of vitality in Chilean poetry. Some of Gabriela Mistral's
poems are *rondas,* a popular form of children's folksongs, and many
of the poems of Neruda were set to music and popularized by Víctor
Jara and Violeta Parra.

The barcarole was a traditional boat song particularly popular
in Venice, where the boatmen used the rhythm to aid in rowing.
It was brought back by Chilean sailors in the nineteenth century
and eventually became part of the anonymous music of folklore.
Neruda's *Barcarole* is divided into three parts, with twelve episodes
that resemble the conversational poetry of *Estravagaria (Extravagaria)*. Even though love is the undisputed center of the book, and
its presence is reinforced by the continuous dialogues with Matilde,
there are also historical episodes praising and poeticizing the lives
of such legendary figures as the Chilean adventurer Joaquín Murieta,
Lord Cochrane, the British captain who reached Valparaíso in the
last century, and Rubén Darío. The poet engages in dialogue with
these heroes—an approach not taken by Neruda in previous works—
and the historical episodes as well as the ahistorical mix harmoni-
ously. Again, Neruda has reserved a place in his poetry for the
balance between the chronicle and the lyric verse. He himself mentions that in this work "no sólo canto sino cuento" ("I not only
sing, I tell').

Barcarole offers a synthesis of the erotic and lyrical cosmic vision
of the love poetry of Neruda. The couple in *Barcarole* is invulnerable
to the threats of the world. Water, sea, and music merge in time,
in the eternity of creative power.

In the figure of the beloved we observe the totality of the universe
and the totality of the life span of the poet. Matilde is the savior
with her "figure of a prow" who guides him, and is his "océana"
(the Spanish word for ocean, which is masculine, made feminine).
She is also the music that consoles the poet and calms him, like a

"spring guitar." All these images found in the poem "Estoy lejos" ("I am Far") reveal that in Neruda's poems the woman symbolizes a reconciliating and harmonizing force. She is everything: her flesh is a ship more powerful than the waves that envelop it. She is also the shadow and the music of earthly clay.

Dorada, la tierra, te dió la armadura del trigo,
el color de los hornos cocieron con barro y delicia,
la piel que no es blanca ni es negra ni es roja ni verde
que tiene el color de la arena, del pan, de la lluvia,
del sol, de la pura madera del viento,
tu carne color de campana, color de alimento fragante,
tu carne que forma la nave y encierra la ola!

(Beloved and golden, earth gave you wheat's armor,
a color that ovens bake in the clays with the sweets and enamels,
that singular skin neither black, white, red nor green
but hued like the sand, the bread crust, the rain,
the sun and the wind and the certain virginal timber,
a flesh, bell colored, colored like savory grains,
yet shaped by a ship's keel and enclosed into a wave!)

("La chascona," *New Decade,* p. 267)

The beloved in *Barcarole* is the essence of many other women represented throughout the amorous lyrics of Pablo Neruda. Music, poetry, and nature converge in this highly lyrical book that is really a pantheist microcosm of the poetic universe of Neruda.

Throughout the *Barcarole* the constant allusion to that *tú* seems to signify the possibility of total integration with "the other." Neruda inverts the traditional theme of love in the barcarole to adapt it to his own creative will. Let us remember that in the folksong the theme of absence and sorrow between the lovers predominates. In Neruda's *Barcarole* love is not represented by estrangement but is closeness and unity. The travel in the voyage of life defies sorrows and terrestrial conflicts.

Chapter Three

The *Residence* Cycle

Neruda and the Avant-Garde

Critics have tended to overlook a vital aspect of Neruda's poetry—his affiliation with the avant-garde movements of the early decades of the century. For Neruda this period culminated in the famous cycle of the *Residences*. Thus, we wish to emphasize that these books do not arise from a vacuum, nor do they derive entirely from Neruda's crushing experiences in the Orient, but rather they are an outgrowth of a poetic tradition that was gestating in Europe as well as Latin America at that time.[1]

In the opinion of many critics, among them Octavio Paz and Saúl Yurkiévich, the Spanish-American modernists—Rubén Darío, Leopoldo Lugones, and Julio Herrera y Reissig, among others—foreshadow the Spanish-American vanguard's use of elaborate images and chaotic enumeration. Yurkiévich summarizes the significance of modernism for the future of Spanish-American poetry: "Modernism proved to be the first literary convergence and the first real internationalization of our poetry. With it appears modernity as our age conceives it: the desire to be in the present, to participate in the progress and expansion of the industrial era."[2]

Spanish-American modernism, with its lyricism and sensuality, its concern for rhythm and sound, and the return to an exotic or Oriental past, inspires a renovation and awakening in the work of the early avant-garde poets: Vicente Huidobro, César Vallejo, the Neruda of *Tentativa del hombre infinito* (Venture of the infinite man, 1926), *El hondero entusiasta* (The ardent Slingsman, 1933), and the *Residences*.

We see that the language of these books, charged with metaphor, intense subjectivity, and distilled aestheticist vocabulary, unleashes the imagination and makes possible a break with the order characterized by logical structures, established rhythms, and other traditional norms of poetic expression.

In Chile Vicente Huidobro pioneers the new poetry declaring that poetic creation must be free from servile imitation of nature. Huidobro is part of a surrealist wave. His art tends towards freedom in the use of metaphor, whose central value lies in the force of the image as access to a superior reality. Huidobro also uses surrealistic techniques such as the disruption of typography. This influence has profound repercussions on the poetry of Neruda, specifically on the writing of the *Residences*.

Let us remember too that in 1922 Vallejo published *Trilce,* one of the fundamental books of the early Spanish-American avant-garde. The poems in *Trilce* appear as an unconnected chain of images in which different modes of written and spoken language converge. The music and magic of language in itself and its attempt to convey the realities of life and experience are entirely fused.

In summary, the early avant-garde, represented by the afore-mentioned three books, is a movement toward liberation, where poetry is not only aesthetic but also participates in a complex system of realities. Fantasy, illusion, and dreams all coexist in the unity of free association and the ideology of a creative style where words take their own course. *Tentativa del hombre infinito* and *El hondero entusiasta* are the initial manifestations of the new concept of poetry and pave the way for the *Residences. Tentativa del hombre infinito* reflects a state of somnambulism and of journeys through fantasy and space. It is the book that, as the author himself said in many interviews, is the least read and studied but one of the most important of his career.

It is in *Tentativa* that Neruda really breaks with traditional poetic forms. As in the writings of the European avant-garde, uncontrolled, fragmentary, and incoherent images predominate. In one poem he writes of a "night of emeralds and windmills." *Tentativa* presents a collection of shimmering images in verses without punctuation that appear to be randomly arranged on the page. The unity of the images lies precisely in their unconnectedness. The absence of punctuation in *Tentativa* is a technique that permits greater freedom of expression and a loosening of the structures imposed by traditional usage, especially in the poems that allude to nocturnal visions. Both James Joyce and Freud can be seen as influences on this use of stream of consciousness technique by Neruda.

In the darkness of night as in the darkness of the poem, sound itself is a means of poetic transport and at the same time a preamble to the night journey that is the central theme of the book. We will observe this quality of poetic phantasmagory fully developed also in "Colección nocturna" and other poems of the *Residences*.

The poem that opens the collection of *Tentativa* is spoken by a man contemplating the sky and the night in a sleeping city. Here as in other poems of *Tentativa*, the narrator of the poem is rapt in the act of contemplation. René de Costa believes that *Tentativa* is based on the idea of the hero's mythic quest.[3] Without disagreeing with de Costa, we may nevertheless develop the idea further, adding that *Tentativa* anticipates many of the tendencies of the Spanish-American avant-garde. The book is "subversive" in the sense of the absolute aesthetic freedom of the lyric speaker in search of the unifying cosmos of man and space. Out of the freedom of the dream-world imagery used by Neruda in *Tentativa* comes the evocation of another facet of dreaming: the nightmare with which the *Residence* cycle begins.

Neruda and the Early Avant-Garde

El hondero entusiasta and *Tentativa del hombre infinito* belong to the so-called transition books that foreshadow a well-defined period within the lyrical production of Neruda. *El hondero* contains resonances and visual images that resemble *Tentativa* especially in the abundant allusions to the oneiric and nocturnal realms.

Previously we said that these two books mark a new stage in Neruda's work because they foreshadow the *Residences* and especially because they introduce the theme of destruction that gains full force in the *Residences*. In *El hondero* those sentiments emerge from the very first verse. We also find the idea of bottomless anguish so typical of the *Residences*, that sense of objects decaying and a world disintegrating.

We may conclude that the first two cycles of *Residence on Earth* climax a poetic process not created in a vacuum but rather unleashed with fury. Neruda had been immersed in a kind of romantic and anguished crisis that also contributed to the atmosphere of the *Residences*. But the great difference between the *Residences* and the earlier books, *Tentativa* and *El hondero* is that in *Residences* intuitive states come together coherently with visceral and physical ones and are projected against a background of objective reality that is seen as a hostile space where existence simply "happens." Instead of rapture, there is an awakening to a pathological external reality that brings about a culmination of Neruda's avant-garde period.

First and Second *Residence*

The volumes entitled *Residence on Earth*[4] have been considered by critics to be among the most important books of Neruda and of Latin American poetry. Numerous critical studies of this work offer a succession of diverse interpretations. For example, one of the most common questions concerns the unity of the work. That is, critics constantly debate the existence of a unifying nucleus in a cycle of poems written over such a long period of time. The first *Residence* covers the period 1925–31, the second 1931–35, and the third 1935–45. We might add that some of the poems of the first *Residence* were composed in Chile between 1935 and 1937 before the poet's trip to the Orient, while others were written entirely in the Orient. As for the *Third Residence* some poems were written in Spain in the period in which Neruda was connected with the poets of the Spanish Resistance against Franco, especially with the group of writers opposed to the extreme aestheticist stance of Juan Ramón Jiménez.

Margarita Aguirre and Héctor Eandi have recently brought to light concrete evidence of Neruda's personal experiences in the Orient through publication of Neruda's letters to Eandi. These letters, so fascinating for their lyrical quality, convincingly document and vividly reflect what Neruda's life was like there. In a letter from Colombo, Ceylon, dated 24 April 1929, he says, regarding the supposed hermeticism of his poetry:

Me he rodeado de una cierta atmósfera secreta, y sufro una verdadera angustia por decir algo, aún solo consigo mismo, como si ninguna palabra me representara, y sufriendo enormemente por ello.

(I have surrounded myself with a certain secret atmosphere and I suffer horribly in order to articulate something, even to myself, as if no word could represent me and I suffer enormously because of it.)[5]

In the *Residences* the vision of decay coincides with the oppressive heat and humidity of Rangoon. The solitude projected in his poetry is the product of all his feelings of alienation in a foreign land. Perhaps the following phrase from the same letter summarizes it best: "Eandi, nadie hay más solo que yo. Recojo perros de la calle,

para acompañarme, pero luego se van, malignos" (Eandi, there is
no one more alone than I. I take in stray dogs to keep me company,
but then they leave me, ungrateful wretches).[6]

A detail that hardly appears in the poems or in the *Memoirs,* and
which we know about only through the letters to Eandi, is the
tremendous difficulty Neruda had in publishing the first *Residence,*
rejected first in Madrid, then in Buenos Aires. We see the desperation of the poet when he receives no answer for years and now it
seems incredible to us. He suffered not only from feelings of terrible
desperation but also from a precarious financial situation and from
the loneliness of the expatriate.

Another revealing letter from Colombo reflects the visceral and
physical misery that surrounds the poet at the time of writing the
first *Residence:* "Cada vez veo menos ideas en torno a mí y más
cuerpos, sol y sudor. Estoy fatigado" (I see fewer and fewer ideas
around me and more and more bodies, sun and sweat. I am besieged).[7]

These introductory remarks show that the cycle of the three *Residences* is motivated by diverse historical experiences: the Spanish
Civil War and personal experiences such as the lonely years in the
Orient. It is clear from what we know of Neruda's life at this time
that the *Residences* grew out of years of intense solitude and
introspection.

This chapter concentrates on the first two volumes of *Residence on
Earth,* which in my opinion constitute a well-defined unity, an
expression of disintegration and nihilism. The *Third Residence* will
be considered separately since its poems evoke a political and social
context that does not coincide with the intimate and personal vision
found in the first two *Residences.*

On reading the first and second *Residences,* we are drawn into a
space inhabited by abandoned and unused objects, dentures left on
dusty dressers, and deserted houses. The techniques characteristic
of *Residence on Earth* are the syncopated use of words, the absence
of adverbs and adjectives, and the constant use of similes that invoke
incongruous images.

For example, in the poem "Galope muerto" ("Dead Gallop") we
see a manifestation of this new poetic style:

> Como cenizas, como mares poblándose,
> en la sumergida lentitud, en lo informe,
> o como se oyen desde lo alto de los caminos.

> (Like ashes, like seas peopling themselves,
> in the submerged slowness, in the shapelessness,
> or as one hears from the crest of the roads.)
>
> ("Dead Gallop," p. 3)

Unexpected images follow each other without logical connections or previous ratiocination. Neruda is no longer writing of the thick forests of the Southern Hemisphere as he did in *Twenty Love Poems,* but of human life on the earth, with all its wretched realities, its absolute defects. The underlying theme of the book is the struggle of the individual who desperately attempts to cease being an outsider among others.

"Dead Gallop" exemplifies the poetic style in the *Residences,* particularly the first *Residence.* There is an absence of adverbs and adjectives, and a resulting vagueness and mystery reinforced by a series of incomplete phrases in the first stanza. The frequent similes have the same effect, as in the first verse: "Como cenizas, como mares poblándose" ("Like ashes, like seas peopling themselves") and set up the pattern of introducing unrelated similes throughout the poem.

The second stanza begins with a demonstrative construction, "Aquello todo" ("All of that") but again this verse has no referent and is followed by incoherent and disordered images. We note the ambiguity of these two verses: "Aquello todo tan rápido, tan viviente / inmóvil sin embargo, como la polea loca en sí misma" ("All that so swift, so living / Yet motionless, like the pulley wild within itself") ("Dead Gallop," p. 3).

The same ambiguity is in evidence throughout the poem, therefore the reader must accept it as a reference to itself, not a composition about a specific theme. Though there are some sensorial references to an external world, they are unprocessed, as if the poet were relating his experiences in a somnambulent and prerational state. This is why the syntax of this poem and others has no special order and the gerundial form is used in a way not usual in the Spanish language, in place of a past participle: "mares poblándose" ("seas peopling themselves").

Many rhetorical questions fill the poem: "Es que por dónde, de dónde, en qué orilla?" ("But from where, through where, on what shore?"). These questions reinforce the stylistic ambiguities found throughout the text and indicate a journey, taken at a galloping pace, which is nonetheless directionless. Words like "dead bees," "black acts," emphasize the metaphysical maladjustment to reality, even as the poem concludes on an optimistic note:

> Adentro del anillo del verano
> una vez los grandes zapallos escuchan
>
> (Within the ring of summer
> once the great calabash trees listen)
> ("Dead Gallop," p. 4)

The word "summer," infrequent in the *Residences,* allows for the regenerative vitality of the earth, while the orange of the calabash contrasts with the predominant grays and blacks of the poem. Yet the poet remains caught in a world hostile and indifferent to him. This poem, besides showing the syntactic construction and the visual images, postulates a philosophy of passivity and submission.

"Ritual de mis piernas" ("Ritual of My Legs") is one of the key poems of this cycle. The poet begins by observing himself, a technique that is discussed by Amado Alonso in his *Poesía y estilo de Pablo Neruda.*[8] Alonso, an authority on Hispanic philology, establishes that Neruda's point of departure is ordinary reality. The poet finds himself encountering a part of his own body:

> Largamente he permanecido mirando mis largas piernas,
> con ternura infinita y curiosa, con mi acostumbrada pasión
> como si hubieran sido las piernas de una mujer divina
> profundamente sumida en el abismo de mi tórax
>
> (For a long time I have stayed looking at my long legs,
> with infinite and curious tenderness, with my accustomed passion,
> as if they had been the legs of a divine woman,
> deeply sunk in the abyss of my thorax)
> ("Ritual of My Legs," p. 73)

The poet experiences an extreme sense of alienation toward his own body, and the lyrical self is objectified. He is a participant who does not try to change or transform the world but to exist in it.

"Ritual of My Legs" is an excellent poem precisely because it objectifies the reality of the speaker, distancing him from his surroundings and even from his own physical self, so that the poet becomes an observer of his own humanity.

The images of the first and second *Residences* are similar in their use of words like "ashes," "fatal," "shadows," "widower," "mourning," "ghosts," "solitude," and "illness". Order collapses, and man, confused and melancholy, remains suspended in impotence. One of the poems that alludes to the state of mind of the poetic speaker is the very well-known "Walking Around," which purposefully chooses an English expression to suggest a state of ambiguity difficult to capture in Spanish: "Sucede que me canso de ser hombre" ("I happen to be tired of being a man") ("Walking Around," p. 118). The lyrical speaker, tired of the city that distances him from his own inner self, uses the expression "sucede," "it happens." Thus the innocuous phrase, constantly repeated, forces us to look at empty establishments, malevolent gardens, and repellent commodities.

The poem begins with an abrupt and decisive force: "tired of being a man" and then continues with a series of enumerations about not wanting to be what he is:

> No quiero sequir siendo raíz en las tinieblas,
> vacilante, extendido, tiritando de sueño
>
> (I don't want to go on being a root in the dark
> vacillating, stretched out, shivering with sleep)
>   ("Walking Around," p. 118)

This poem is of particular interest because the poet's "walking around" indicates a vague sleep-walking motion amidst decrepit objects like old coffee pots and soiled clothing. This same reverberation of solitude and sadness comes through in almost all of the poems of these *Residences* that are, as is often said, residences in hell.

The lyrical speaker is identified with a felt swan that contrasts with the precious swan used so often by the Spanish-American modernists, especially Darío. The faded swan made of swatches of cloth does not float on a crystalline lake but on a sea of "origin and ashes," of birth and of death. The third stanza announces not only the sense of loneliness accentuated by the urban environment but also the rejection of his own body, his fingernails, feet, and the reflection of himself as a shadow:

> Sucede que me canso de mis pies y mis uñas
> y mi pelo y mi sombra.
> Sucede que me canso de ser hombre.

> (I happen to be tired of my feet and my nails
> and my hair and my shadow.
> I happen to be tired of being a man.)
>   ("Walking Around," p. 118)

He speaks of "frightening a notary with a lily," a bit of fantasy in which the notary would represent legality and calcified life in opposition to the lyrical object, a cut lily. The poet wishes to eradicate the banality of existence by means of spontaneous actions that would throw into disorder the accepted behaviors of every day. The same idea of defiance is reiterated in the image of "killing a nun," this time directed towards institutionalized religion:

> Sin embargo sería delicioso
> asustar a un notario con un lirio cortado
> o dar muerte a una monja con un golpe de oreja.
> Sería bello
> ir por las calles con un cuchillo verde
> y dando gritos hasta morir de frío.

> (Nevertheless it would be delightful
> to startle a notary with a cut lily
> or kill a nun with a blow to the ear.
> It would be lovely
> to go through the streets with a sexy knife
> and shouting until I froze to death.)
>   ("Walking Around," p. 118)

After a series of hypothetical suppositions of what would be lovely instead of what is, the poet uses the symbol of the knife or sword, so often used in the *Residences* in association with elementary things like stones and roses as a symbolic expression of adventure. The sexy knife recalls the oneiric and surrealistic images of Lorca that invoke a somnambulent and magical state. Thus the verse "ir por las calles con un cuchillo verde dando gritos hasta morir de frío" displaces the rational realm with a phantasmagory.

The poem continues with a series of images that refer back to the first stanzas and reinforce the apathy and disenchantment with external reality. Gradually there emerges the idea of disintegration and lost life with allusions to "horribles intestinos" ("horrible intestines") and "dentaduras abandonadas en cafeteras" ("dentures abandoned in coffee pots"), that is, repellent objects left in alien places.

Only once does the lyrical speaker find what he is seeking: "un descanso de piedras o de lana" ("a respite of stones or wool"), stones evoking tranquillity and eternity and wool for softness and warmth—images that represent a profound rejection of hostile elements that enchain.

Poems like "Melancolía en las familias" ("Melancholy in Families"), "Enfermedades en mi casa" ("Illnesses in My House"), and "Sólo la muerte" ("Only Death") are essential poems that allude to that state of helplessness and existence where even objects begin to disintegrate. Even a walk through the city becomes a vision of mire and death.

Paradoxically, the unity of the *Residences* lies in the process of disintegration, expressed by bold images, enjambment of words, and rhythmic and musical tonality. Another important poem that exemplifies the techniques of disintegration is "Ars poética" ("Ars Poetica"). The poem is a single interminable phrase of strangely combined images situated in no particular place: the line "entre sombra y espacio, entre guarniciones y doncellas" ("between shadow and space, between trimmings and damsels") ("Ars Poetica," p. 46) produces a strange sense of indetermination and ambiguity, but then the images multiply, and the lexicon connotes depression and decrepitude: "tengo la misma sed ausente y la misma fiebre fría" ("I have the same absent thirst and the same cold fever") ("Ars Poetica," p. 46).

Another characteristic of these poems is the use of unfinished comparisons. We do not know what is being compared with what. The poem also maintains a series of unanswered questions: "quién amó lo perdido, quién protegió lo último?" ("who loved the lost, who protected the last?") ("Sonata y destruciones," "Sonata and Destructions," p. 52)—rhetorical questions that facilitate that state of high tension characteristic of the *Residences.*

The reader may well ask what motivated the poet to change so drastically from his luminous *Crepusculario* phase to the stunning beauty of *Twenty Love Poems* and then abruptly to the definitive break of the *Residences.* In the journal *Caballo verde para la poesia* (Green horse for poetry),[9] published in Madrid in 1935, a joint creation of

Neruda and Rafael Alberti, Neruda wrote a manifesto entitled "Towards an Impure Poetry" in which many critics have found the key
to understanding the *Residences:* "Es muy conveniente en ciertas horas
del día o de la noche, observar profundamente los objetos en descanso: las ruedas que han recorrido largas, polvorientas distancias."
(It is good at certain hours of the day or night, to look closely at
the world of objects at rest: wheels that have crossed long dusty
distances). [10]

The phrase "objects" refers to Neruda's extensive use of ephemeral
things, such as broken mirrors and abandoned houses. Nothing
escapes the poet's reach and everything can be part of the poetic
act. Nothing eludes the avid gaze of the poet. In "Widower's Tango"
he speaks even of the empty shoes he left behind when escaping his
lover Josie Bliss and of grimy coffee pots. He does not elevate or
mythify these things, but describes them as object that constitute
daily reality.

It is relevant here that decades later, in the nineteen fifties, Neruda
continues to pay close attention to isolated objects. All things are
a source of lyrical expression: onions, dictionaries, book bindings,
and artichokes. But in the *Odes* these objects will be discovered with
a feeling of kinship, joy, and participation in a suddenly hospitable
earth. Man-made objects such as cups and plates become participants
in the ritual of life. But in the *Residences* Neruda sings of objects
and substances in disuse, of the unaesthetic face of life.

The unifying symbiosis of nature acts as an accomplice of the
poet. For example, in "Debilidad del alba" ("The Dawn's Debility")
the formless rain appears as a gray substance reflecting the decaying
external world: "La lluvia cae sobre mí, y se me parece" ("The rain
falls upon me and it seems like me") ("The Dawn's Debility," p.
12).

It is important to bear in mind that the two *Residences* were written
sporadically, not only in the Orient but also in Chile and Spain.
The writing of the *Residences* coincides with a crisis in Western
culture of the post-war period, as well as with the personal conflicts
experienced by the poet. While modernism, the first international
poetic movement born in Spanish-American territory, reacted against
the decadence of values motivated by the Industrial Revolution and
was an escape into aestheticism, the poetry of Neruda responds to
decay by confronting it.

To cite the work of Spanish critic Amado Alonso again, Alonso was the first to study in depth the style of the *Residences* and to point out the symbolist influences. Alonso emphasizes the overwhelming desolation, manifested through stylistic dislocations. Some modifications of Alonso's work have already been suggested by such critics as Emir Rodríguez Monegal, Jaime Concha, and others[11] who believe that *Residence* is indeed a poetry of disintegration, but that within that disintegration there is also a combative spirit and the presence of a will to resurrect hope.

Let us recall that even "Walking Around," with its reiterations and enumerations of ennui, nonetheless contains elements of humor: "Si pudiéramos asustar a un notario" ("If only we could frighten a notary"). "Dead Gallop", too, terminates with an optimistic note, saying that:

> Adentro del anillo del verano
> una vez los grandes zapallos escuchan,
> estirando sus plantas conmovedoras
>
> (Within the ring of summer
> Calabash trees once listen,
> stretching out their pity-laden plants)
> ("Dead Gallop," p. 4)

The possibility of regeneration still exists in nature, an important aspect that should not be overlooked in the study of the *Residences*.

Alonso touches upon another point that is worthy of elaboration—that these poems should not be approached with rigid interpretations, but should be regarded as manifestations of prelogical and intuitive apprehension of the real world. The fact that the *Residences* were written as if in a state prior to organized cognition constitutes the very essence and explains the hermetic nature of the work. Both in Huidobro and in Neruda we see writing being liberated from grammatical bonds and flowing naturally. Such is the legacy of surrealism in Latin America.

Manuel Durán, in the previously mentioned book *Earth Tones*, also insists that these poems must be "grasped intuitively rather than logically defined by the conscious mind."[2] From this intuitive view of reality, expressed by an anomalous syntax, full of incomplete prepositions and absent adverbs, is born the language of *Residence on Earth*. The elusive language of *Residence* makes it a unique book that paradoxically conveys disintegration and at the same time a wish for regeneration.

Many poems reinforce this idea, for example, "Colección nocturna" ("Nocturnal Collection") where the oneiric element and the unreal stand out palpably throughout the poem. In "Nocturnal Collection" the immense power of imagination reveals to us that the poet is attempting to penetrate the multiple spheres of the subconscious like a seer trying to name and describe through images that are mysteriously subjective and imprecise. The haunting world of dreams takes hold of the speaker and torments him. He sees cruel-faced women and tearless friends in a vision that reappears to him in a state of wakefulness.

This oneiric and surrealistic vision is repeated over and over in *Residence,* as in the poem "Caballo de sueño" ("Dream Horse"), which speaks of the flavor of dreaming as the essential substance of the poem. Another oneiric composition is "El fantasma del buque de carga" ("Ghost of the Freight Ship"), which creates the impression of a demential and solitary walk through an abandoned ship. The stricken speaker tells us what happened during that mysterious tour, as he roamed through the hold, among sacks like shadowy animals, round, and eyeless. The poet himself is part of this vision of a chaotic world where the images of the poems seem like flashes of the oneiric world. The night represents not terror but the possibilities of imagination, as in the works of André Bréton and Guillaume Apollinaire.

As the poem closes, the poet describes a vast country of rainbows and lush vegetation and tells of dreaming among those plants. An air of impurity surrounds and submerges him, yet he desires "a bolt of lightning" to return him to the reconciling light of nature. We consider this poem fundamental because it captures the idea of the decomposition of matter and at the same time the desire for unity with imperishable beauty. At the end of the *Residence,* a reordered world returns.

"Tres cantos materiales"
("Three Material Songs")

The "Material Songs"—"Entrada a la madera" ("Entry into the Wood"), "Apogeo del apio" ("The Apogee of Celery"), and "Estatuto del vino" ("The Ordinance of Wine")—seemingly fall outside of the poetic sequence of disintegration we have seen in the *Residences*. While the fundamental poems of the *Residences* evoke disintegration of urban reality, "Tres cantos materiales," appropriately placed at the end of the second *Residence,* represent a respite from these hallucinated visions.

Wood is perhaps one of the most important images that Neruda carries from the beginning of his poetry to the end. Wood takes him back to early childhood, to the great lumberyards of Temuco. As he says: "Es que soy yo ante tu color de mundo" ("I am the one facing your worldly color") ("Entry into the Wood," p. 155). It is this inviting fragrance, this material, defined as "sweet matter" and "rose with dry wings" that the poet seeks in his first song. Nature, exemplified by the image of wood, allows a return to the mythical past of his childhood. [13]

This poem differs from the poems of the *Residence,* because the external setting of nature is a positive refuge that consoles the poet for his "lamentos sin origen" ("laments without origin") and attempts to assimilate him in that primary universe.

"Entrada a la madera" describes the physical journey of a speaker immersed in the atmosphere of the *Residences,* an atmosphere of mourning, until the "entrada" "entry," or the return to matter. The components of wood are traced in detail—pores, veins, circles of sweetness—until the poet loses himself in them. It is this longing to be part of primary substances that Neruda tries to bring back at the end of the *Residence* cycle.

Confidence in the harmonious regeneration of man and nature is also evident in the second song, "Apogeo del apio" ("Apogee of Celery") in which, like "Entrada a la madera," the decadent external world is replaced by the creative and restorative capacity of plants. Celery, like wood, is a metaphor for material substances. In this song, there is a detailed description of the physionomy of celery, with its little veins, and its top hat, transformed into a dancing figure that enters the open markets. The personification of celery is the first foreshadowing of the *Odes.* Celery is the mother earth whose magic powers give life:

> Río de vida y hebras esenciales,
> verdes ramas de sol acariciado,
> aquí estoy, en la noche, escuchando secretos,
> desvelos, soledades,

> y entraís, en medio de la niebla hundida,
> hasta crear en mí, hasta comunicarme
> la luz oscura y la rosa de la tierra.
>
> (River of life and essential fibers,
> green branches of cherished sun,
> here I am, in the night, listening to secrets,
> wakefulness, solitudes,
> and you enter, amid the sunken fog,
> until you grow in me, until you reveal to me
> the dark light and the rose of the earth.)
>   ("Apogee of Celery," p. 160)

The same concept of involvement with roots, whether wood or vegetable, emerges again in these two poems filled with the longing for return. Even the dialogues between celery and the poet allude to this empathy of man and nature. Through evocations and nostalgia Neruda finds the lost integration with nature. In the final song, "Estatuto del vino," we shall see how the integration takes place through fellow men.

"The Ordinance of Wine" initiates a break with the two previous poems, since here we see the poet again involved with the decrepit reality of other men. Wine is seen as part of a precarious world of canals, suns, and humid streets where wine reaches all people. It is a duplicitous liquid that is both a product of creation and of destruction.

The images in the poem are sharply realistic. The smell of feet, shoes, and grapes in the scene of men at a bar is a double image that alludes to the barefoot men making wine and to the drunk men wearing shoes. Despite their intoxication, they are linked with all mortals, "golpeando el ataúd con un hueso de pájaro" ("striking the coffin with a bird bone") ("Ordinance of Wine," p. 165), perhaps sensing their own deaths. When man comes into contact with the natural substance of wine, it loses its initial purity and becomes part of the persecution of men.

Although the "Cantos materiales" resemble the poems of Gabriela Mistral entitled "Elogios de las cosas de tierra" (Praise of earthly things), with respect to the awareness of physical substances, there is a break with the mythification Mistral projects onto nature.

Whether Neruda's relationship to natural substances is a religious communion or a pantheistic one, as critics have suggested, these three songs illustrate his concept of fusion between man and nature.

Third Residence

In "El estatuto del vino," one particular verse reveals clearly the poet's new stance and anticipates the new aesthetic and lyrical mode of the *Third Residence,* composed between 1935 and 1945:

> Hablo de cosas que existen. Dios me libre
> de inventar cosas cuando estoy cantando.

> (I speak of things that exist. Heaven forbid
> that I should invent things when I am singing.)
> ("Ordinance of Wine," p. 165)

The *Third Residence* consists of five sections organized by themes, the first one centered on an obsession with solitude. The poem "Vals" ("Waltz") is a good example of that sense of alienation outlined in the earlier works. The poet says: "No soy no sirvo no conozco a nadie" ("I am not, I am no good. I don't know anyone") ("Waltz," p. 219).

The essential merit of this collection, according to the majority of critics, lies in the political, social, and ethical content of the poems found in the section *España en el corazón,* including the extensive "Canto a Bolívar" ("Song to Bolívar") and "Nuevo canto a Stalingrado" ("New Song to Stalingrad"). The force of this book, then, lies principally in the poems of a political nature. Neruda is no longer the intensely introspective poet of the earlier period but the active participant and narrator of concrete events: the Spanish Civil War and the Second World War. We see clearly the influence on young Neruda of the poets of the so-called Generation of 27— Lorca, Guillén, Alberti—the group that revives interest in Golden Age writers such as Quevedo and Góngora whom these poets choose as their guide and inspiration.

Neruda has acknowledged an avid interest in Quevedo, whose "Cartas y sonetos de la muerte" (Letters and sonnets of death) he included in the 25 July 1935 issue of *Cruz y Raya* (Cross and ray). In Quevedo, Neruda found a powerful stimulus that brought him back to his Hispanic heritage. Quevedo, so deeply involved in the

politics and history of his time, serves as a model for Neruda. The
poet confesses his profound admiration for a man who condemned
the corruption and the decadence of seventeenth-century Spain without renouncing his vitality and love of life.

With these observations in mind, we shall proceed to the fundamental poems of the *Third Residence*. In "El abandonado" ("The
Abandoned One") Neruda seeks the common man, who will be the
subject of future works. This poem foreshadows the "Ode to Invisible
Man" that reflects the same concern:

> Yo no sé: yo sólo sufro de no saber
> quien eres
>
> (I do not know: I only suffer from not
> knowing who you are)
> ("The Abandoned One," p. 223)

On this plane of daily reality we find the core of the *Third Residence*.
Neruda's attention is now focused on living men rather than on
disintegrating things. One of the best-known poems of *Spain in My
Heart* is the poem "Explico algunas cosas" ("I Explain a Few Things"),
which has been seen as a manifesto of his new stance.[14] The poem
begins with a number of indirect questions:

> Preguntaréis: ¿Y dónde están las lilas?
> ¿Y la metafísica cubierta de amapolas?
> ¿Y la lluvia que a menudo golpeaba
> sus palabras llenándolas
> de agujeros y pájaros?
>
> (You will ask: And where are the lilacs?
> And the metaphysical blanket of poppies
> And the rain that often struck
> Your words filling them
> With holes and birds?)
> ("I Explain a Few Things," p. 255)

These queries immediately establish a direct communication with
the reader that did not occur in the earlier *Residences*. These verses
imply that the beauty of the lilacs and the melancholy rain no longer

exist. The poet's dialogue with himself has ceased, and he speaks directly to his readers and listeners, telling and singing his story with musical rhythm, even nursery rhyme rhythm. This necessity of involving the audience with the poet is a radical departure from the earlier works—from *Crepusculario* to *Residences*.

The poem continues with daily situations, ordinary descriptions, and no hermeticism or imagistic complexity:

> Yo vivía en un barrio
> de Madrid con campanas,
> relojes, con árboles.
>
> (I lived in a quarter
> of Madrid, with bells
> with clocks, with trees.)
> ("I Explain a Few Things," p. 255)

Then he begins to enumerate all the objects that are in that house. He makes one allusion to Castile, described as a "dry face," a metaphor that gives us his vision of Spain. The colloquial tone resumes, as he calls to his fellow poets and readers.

In an intimate appellative tone he speaks to his friends: to Federico García Lorca, already murdered and buried in an unmarked grave, and to the already exiled Rafael Alberti. Neruda begins to remember the past beauty of Alberti's house and contrasts it to the abandoned house of the present. This memory is necessary in order to re-create a Spain that no longer exists, a Spain full of prosperity and happiness in contrast to a decaying Spain surrounded by the horrors of war.

"I Explain a Few Things" presents the image of a Spain full of laughter, flowers, children. Gradually, though, the images of light and abundance begin to fade and are replaced by the image of war. The poetic shift begins with the verse "y una mañana todo estaba ardiendo." Fire as a symbol of violence and destruction will dominate the rest of the poem. The final stanza is a militant cry:

> Venid a ver la sangre por las calles,
> venid a ver
> la sangre por las calles
> venid a ver la sangre
> por las calles!

> (Come and see the blood in the streets
> come and see
> the blood in the streets
> come and see the blood
> in the streets!)
> ("I Explain a Few Things," p. 260)

Here the personal story of the poet on Arguelles Street becomes a collective experience and his burnt house an emblem for a divided Spain. Neruda uses a rhythm such as that used in declamatory poetry, with repetition accentuating the themes. For example, the constant repetition of "venid a ver." A technique that is repeated in the section *Spain in My Heart* is the combining of narration with the techniques of oral poetry. The same phenomenon can be seen in another poem, "Como era España" ("What Spain Was Like").

Other poems denounce the aggression committed by Franco's forces. Neruda condemns the decadent Spain "vestida de asma y huecos levitones sangrientos" ("dressed in asthma and bloody hollow frock coats") ("La tradición," "Tradition," p. 253). In speaking of a decadent tradition he also proposes a new world of hope and solidarity.

As the political consciousness of the poet awakens, he finds reasons for alliance with other men and especially with the common people. "Reunión bajo las nuevas banderas" ("Meeting under New Flags") is a key poem that accentuates the concept of solidarity, by the words "together," "reunited," "new flags," and the exhortation "together against sorrow."

But Neruda's political concerns are not only limited to Spain but reach out to other countries, as in the moving poem "Canto a los ríos de Alemania" ("Song to the Rivers of Germany"), which expresses compassion for people victimized and marked by the sinister past of their own country. The poem uses a popular form of the nursery rhyme with a refrain, "El Rhin en la noche" ("The Rhine at Night"), which is easily remembered, thus establishing a comforting link with childhood songs. The poem's end proclaims a new determination:

> y desde la desdicha sus aguas se levantan.
> La voz secreta crece junto a las rojas márgenes
> y el hombre sumergido se levanta y camina.

(and from the misfortune its waters rise.
The secret voice grows next to the red banks
and the sunken man rises up and walks.)
("Song to the Rivers of Germany," p. 342)

Perhaps one of the most significant poems of *Third Residence* is the "Un canto a Bolívar" ("A Song to Bolívar"), which begins in the form of "The Lord's Prayer." Here Bolívar is invoked as the guardian and advocate of Latin American unity. Written in 1914, with Europe at war, and recited in postrevolutionary Mexico, the poem had many implications of a new resurgence of Latin America. Neruda speaks of an imagined encounter with Bolívar:

Yo conocí a Bolívar una mañana larga,
en Madrid, en la boca del Quinto Regimiento,
Padre, le dije, eres o no eres o quién eres?

(I came upon Bolívar, one long morning,
In Madrid, at the entrance to the Fifth Regiment,
Father, I said to him, are you, or are you not, or who are you?)
("Song to Bolívar," p. 337)

Some of the poetry found in the *Residences* has been considered by many as propaganda and perhaps for this reason has been neglected by critics. Although Neruda presents his political beliefs in these books, we cannot fail to see that in these poems, political and social in content, Neruda is still introducing new poetic techniques that have great significance for the development of his poetry.

In the last *Residence* Neruda goes through a kind of lyrical resurrection. Obsessed in the *Twenty Love Poems* with the beloved and preoccupied in the earlier *Residences* with the disintegration of manmade spaces, he arrives at the *Third Residence* feverishly renewed. The vocabulary of images in decomposition, so frequent before, take on a new vitality because the poet's experience in Spain, the mother country, stirs his roots and helps him to view his continent. Each phase of Neruda's poetry leads to another: after the affective hermeticism of *Twenty Love Poems* and the stylistic hermeticism of the two *Residences*, Neruda reveals himself once more as the poet who flowers and sings with a refreshed voice.

Las furias y las penas

Despite the fact that *Las furias y las penas (The Furies and the Sorrows)* appears as part of the *Third Residence,* this long poem does not share the most fundamental theme of the book, which comes out of a social and political consciousness. Nonetheless, it is interesting to place it within this process of Neruda's evolution. He himself tells us in the introduction to this narrative poem:

> En 1934 fue escrito este poema. Cúantas cosas han sobrevivido desde entonces! España, donde lo escribí, es una cintura de ruinas. Ay! si con sólo una gota de poesía o de amor pudiéramos aplacar la ira del mundo, pero eso sólo lo pueden la lucha y el corazón resuelto.
>
> El mundo ha cambiado y mi poesía ha cambiado. Una gota de sangre caída en estas lineas quedará viviendo sobre ellas, indeleble como el amor.

(This poem was written in 1934. How many things have come to pass since then! Spain, where I wrote it, is a circle of ruins. Ah, if with only a drop of poetry or love we could placate the anger of the world, but that can be done only by striving and by a resolute heart.

The world has changed and my poetry has changed. A drop of blood fallen on these lines will remain living upon them, indelible as love.)
(Residence on Earth, p. 230)

As the Quevedo-like title indicates, the poem tells the story of a furious and tragic love. Nowhere else in Neruda is there such verbal eroticism as in this poem, which shares in the chaotic world of the earlier *Residences* because sex offers no type of refuge. On the contrary, it is a perpetual corporeal struggle that finally dies and covers the poet with ashes.

The beloved, who before appeared as a safe port against the evils of the world and whose body was in harmony with nature, is now an enemy. Sex without love is the basic recurrent motif of the poem. The adolescent girl of the green eyes and gray beret is now a violent animal lying in wait because the female body means annihilation instead of union. The word "juntos" ("together") means the very opposite, separation, and the agony of the couple's solitude is motivated by the erotic impulse.

The Furies and the Sorrows has a historical importance in the lyrical trajectory of the poet. First, it is one of the great erotic poems written by Neruda, but it is also drastically different from the other amorous poems because of the crude images used. The sexual encounters occur in dirty rooms decorated with velvet covered by excrement, a nauseating space where man and woman appear as objects of no importance:

> Yo era un hombre transportado al acaso,
> con una mujer hallada vagamente,
> nos desnudamos
> como para morir o nadar o envejecer
> y nos metimos uno dentro del otro
>
> (I was a man transported by chance,
> with a woman vaguely found,
> we undressed
> as if to die or swim or grow old
> and we thrust ourselves one inside the other)
> (*The Furies and the Sorrows*, p. 239)

The encounter is a form of closure for the couple, and love is not part of a cycle of regeneration but of total destruction. In this way, *The Furies and the Sorrows* corresponds to the cycle of *Residence* whose theme is finality. The lexical construction of this poem has to do with that chaotic world, an ambivalent universe where the sexual encounter is both horrorific and fascinating. The brothel scenes and the overlap of disconnected images all tie in with the earlier *Residences*.

This poem, which represents the sterility of love and the lack of communication with the beloved, brings to a close an important phase of Neruda's poetry. After *The Furies and the Sorrows* Neruda's love poetry will change once more in *The Captain's Verses,* where love becomes once again an integrating force.

Chapter Four

Canto General: The Word and the Song of America

Within the context of Chilean lyric poetry, there is a precedent for Neruda's next work, the *Canto general:* the sixteenth-century epic poem *La Araucana,*[1] written by a Spaniard, Alfonso Ercilla y Zúñiga. This epic poem represents a foundation work on the subject of Chilean poetic history, presented in a lyrical form. Here we find Chile's splendorous geography and its valiant native inhabitants. Pablo Neruda, like previous Spanish-American poets such as Rubén Darío and José Santos Chocano, revives the broken epic tradition with one of the most important poems from his pen: *Canto general* or General song.

The idea for the poem developed over a period of time and can be traced from the epoch of *Spain in My Heart* when Neruda began to turn his attention to his own land and his own people. According to Rodríguez Monegal, Neruda started to compose *Canto general* in 1938, the year of his father's death.[2] At first dedicated exclusively to Chile under the title *Canto de Chile* (Song of Chile), it was a collection of geographical, historical, and political descriptions of his country. Significant in terms of literary parallels is the fact that in this same period, Gabriela Mistral began to write her own nostalgic *Canto de Chile,* in which the poet imagines herself traversing the long, slender Chilean territory on the back of a *huemul.* (The *huemul* is an animal indigenous to South America and similar to the horse.)

In 1938, when the initial idea of *Canto general* and especially the *Canto de Chile* was evolving, Neruda was engaged in fervent political activity. In 1940 he was posted to Mexico as Chilean consul and in this period, according to the critic Fernando Alegría,[3] he wrote the section "América, no invoco tu nombre en vano" (America, I do not invoke your name in vain), "Oratorio menor en la muerte de Silvestre Revueltas" (Minor oratorio upon the death of Silvestre

Revueltas), and "En los muros de México" (On the walls of Mexico), poems that later formed an essential part of the *Canto general*.

Another important year for the evolution of the *Canto general* was 1946. In that year, the order for Neruda's arrest was issued by the government headed by President González Videla; it is then that Neruda wrote another autobiographical segment of the *Canto general*, "El fugitivo." This persecution forced Neruda to take refuge in humble homes and permitted him to live with the ordinary Chilean people.

Before returning to Mexico in 1943, Neruda visited the ruins of Macchu Picchu (the lost city of the Incas, discovered in 1911 by an American archeologist, Hiram Bingham, from Yale University). The ruins of that once powerful empire are a magnificent symbol of the glorious pre-Columbian past of Hispanic America. Neruda was inspired by a desire to identify with that native American past: "Me sentí chileno, peruano, americano. Había encontrado en aquellas alturas difíciles, entre aquellas ruinas gloriosas y dispersas, una profesión de fé para la continuación de mi canto" (I felt Chilean, Peruvian, American. I had found in those harsh heights, among dispersed and glorious ruins, a profound faith in the continuation of my song).[4]

The visit to the citadel at Macchu Picchu is of capital importance in understanding the *Canto general*. Neruda himself affirms that this experience expanded his horizons and his sense of being a part of the American continent. He began to identify not only with Chile but with all of America. *Las alturas de Macchu Picchu (The Heights of Macchu Picchu)* was written in Chile in 1945 at Isla Negra, overlooking the sea. In 1950 an expensive limited edition of this long poem, which, as we have said, had been developing since 1938, was published. Thus it is not, as critics have often claimed, a quickly dashed-off poetic treatise of political ideology. It is, on the contrary, a carefully crafted poem that took twelve years to compose.

Neruda was becoming increasingly committed to social issues that he addressed through his writing and was moving towards an identification with the long oppressed and exploited working class of Latin America. In the section "Las flores de Punitaqui" (The flowers of Punitaqui) Neruda describes the economic and social problems of the miners and their strikes against subhuman working conditions. An example of this is the poem dedicated to Cristóbal Miranda, which denounces the perils of the saltpeter mines. Another is the well-known poem "The United Fruit Company," which makes explicit reference to foreign colonizers as perpetuators of evils that are centuries old. These examples are an indication that Neruda is becoming increasingly oriented towards achieving a political purpose that goes beyond pure aesthetics.

The final sections of the *Canto general* identify class problems as a legitimate preoccupation of the poet, who believes in the liberating power of the word. The aforementioned section "Las flores de Punitaqui" of the poem "Hermano Pablo" (Brother Pablo) evinces with unusual clarity the desire to address the proletarians whose lives form the thematic substance of the poem. The peasants come to "Hermano Pablo" asking for basic necessities: water, food, and shelter. Neruda tries to respond to the injust legacy of hunger by identifying himself with the struggle of the people. This poem, and others like it, abandons the earlier rhetoric of introspection in order to confront a collective reality.

Neruda's Marxist ideology combines as idealistic materialism with the central theme of the relationships between man, the land, and history. As Eduardo Camacho writes in his book *Pablo Neruda: Naturaleza, historia y poética,*[5] Neruda integrates dialectical materialism with historical materialism. These two dimensions are complementary since from the beginning, American nature appears in all its splendor on the visual plane, and man's place in it is firmly established. Thus, the poet assumes the task of constructing with his verse a new society of men conscious of their connections with the land and the products of their labor.

Marxist materialism in the *Canto general* is most evident in the poem *The Heights of Macchu Picchu* whose final section invokes a rebirth of man. This rebirth is also expressed as redemption in poems such as "La huelga" (The strike) in the section "Las flores de Punitaquí," which also presents a Marxist component. In the first part there is a class struggle in which the poor are identified as the oppressed. In the second part the people unite in their struggle and resist. The third and final part, like the last section of *The Heights of Macchu Picchu,* implies a rebirth, a future, and the hope of a people united: "Hay un mensaje escrito en sus paredes / y sólo el pueblo puede verlo" (There is a message written on the walls / and only the people can read it).[6] History is reconstructed and redeemed by the workers themselves. They become the authors of a new destiny, breaking the cycle of perpetual colonization. Neruda also assumes the role as mediator to the people since he cedes his own voice to "the other."

It would be impossible to speak of Neruda without mentioning his political engagement with Latin America. Throughout the *Canto general* there is a clear Marxist tendency that has bolstered Neruda's reputation among partisans of this political camp. In this complex poem, Neruda brings into harmony a poetic chronicle of Latin American history and the Marxist interpretation of human development. According to Hernán Loyola, Neruda is faced with two objectives that could be contradictory, [he]

opts for a poetic representation founded more on popular folk tradition than on historical rigor. . . . This seemingly reductive . . . operation permits the functional elaboration, in an epic key, of a mythical design which ultimately succeeds in joining the most profound Americanist intuition of the poet to the level of accessibility and combative efficacy that the historical moment demands.[7]

Canto general narrates the history of a people colonized first by the Spaniards and later by other modern powers such as the foreign multinationals described as being allies of dictators who betray their own countries. Oppression on the American continent is defined as emanating from capitalism, and redemption is seen in Marxism, two antagonistic forces. Liberation comes at the end of the *Canto general* when the people speak for themselves, and the terrible apocalypse is avoided. Poetry, history, and ideology come together in a collective canto that is also deeply personal.

Canto general is one of the most ambitious works written by Neruda or by any Spanish-American poet. Margarita Aguirre's thoughtful biography, *Las vidas de Pablo Neruda*,[8] tells us that Neruda spent a great deal of time searching out the numerous historical references that he deliberately worked into the poem and then worked eight to ten hours daily in writing the book.

The *Canto general,* published in Mexico and illustrated by the great muralists Diego Rivera and David Alfaro Siqueiros, cannot be considered a work isolated from the others, for the concerns of this poem are paralleled by many midcentury analytical essays on Latin American reality by such important writers as the Colombian Germán Arciniegas, as well as Alfonso Reyes and Octavio Paz, both Mexicans.

According to René de Costa in *The Poetry of Pablo Neruda*,[9] the Paz essay represents a meditation on Mexican culture and Neruda's a mythification of the American continent. Like the majority of critics, de Costa believes that *Canto general* is in itself a mythical exaltation of American culture. Other critics, like Fernando Alegría and Rodríguez Monegal, believe that it is an ideological exaltation with definite colors. The heroes are the Indians, original inhabitants of these lands, and the antiheroes are first the Spanish colonizers and, later, the North Americans who, with the United Fruit Company, invade the "banana republics."

Although we can agree that these concepts are indeed prevalent in *Canto general,* it would be a mistake to stop here. For a deeper understanding of the tone and structure of *Canto general,* we must analyze it as a lyric totality and examine especially the ideological and social components. The richness of the text lies in the abundance of its interpretive possibilities and in the variety of its images and styles.

Canto general, as the title indicates, is a comprehensive song, a hymn to a continent in which the poet expresses the historical and social vision of the American people. It connects this history to a past, present, and future, interweaving, with magnificent harmony and sensitivity, cosmogonies invented by the poet himself, like those we see in the first section of the book, "La lámpara en la tierra," (The lamp on earth). We also see historical meditations of a contemporary conscience as in the section "La arena traicionada" (Sand betrayed) or "Los libertadores" (The liberators).

To create this amalgamation of lyrical coordinates Neruda chose the epic tone, like the medieval minstrel who speaks for others in telling a story. It is interesting to note the perfect balance between the early sections of *Las alturas de Macchu Picchu* in which Neruda says: "Yo vengo a hablar por vuestra boca muerta" (I come to speak through your dead mouth) and at the end of the *Canto:* "Y nacerá de nuevo esta palabra" (And this word will be born once again); that is, the story will be reconstructed and retold by others to come later.

Canto general alternates two speakers, the poet-singer and the poet-historian, who re-create the history and vision of the American continent, not from the point of view of official accounts, however, but rather from a new poetic perspective. The protagonists in this new history are miners, farmers, Indians, and other ordinary people who rarely appear in official history books. The personal and the collective are intertwined with the detailed description of the flora and fauna. Neruda's definition of an epic, as seen in the *Canto general*, coincides with that of Ezra Pound who saw it as "a poem with history in it" and regarded his own *Cantos* as an epic.

In *Canto general*, Neruda concentrates on the stories of those who have no voice, "invisible men," so that the poem becomes the collective chronicle of a people. Neruda, like Walt Whitman, is a minstrel who transmits as well as transforms the history of his continent.

The personal element in this work is inevitable because, though Neruda sings and recounts the collective history of America, the voice is his own. To the "objective" history of Latin America he adds his own subjectivity.

In *Canto general* we observe a constant dichotomy between the indigenous peoples, true heirs to the land, and the conquistadores who are invaders. This sharp division has been the subject of criticism for what can be called dogmatism in Neruda. Though his characters are indeed divided into heroes and villains, the *Canto* as a whole is still one of the finest epic poems in the Spanish language.

The poem is divided into fifteen sections whose tonal and thematic variety is its greatest achievement. Despite the variety each poem finds its place within the lyrical structure and within the historical and social context of the poem.

Saúl Yurkievich, in his excellent study, *Fundadores de la nueva poesía hispanoamericana*,[10] suggests a new reading of the *Canto general*. Yurkievich says that the break with organized images and metaphoric conceptualization in the verses of this long poem, especially in the first section, "La lámpara en la tierra," indicates a state of intuitive imagination that merges with ancestral history. The language of the poet is ever more closely linked to his material, to the organic substances of the land he is describing. Even in the section "Yo soy" (I am) he says: "Dadme todas las cosas de la tierra" (Give me all the things of the earth) (p. 429), and then his whole being becomes immersed in this original substance.

Canto general derives from the same personal poetics of the humid Chilean South, a poetics that expands imagistically throughout the Latin American continent, like the tree that is its constant symbol in the text.

"La lámpara en la tierra" (The lamp on earth)

The first part of the *Canto general,* entitled "La lámpara en la tierra," immediately establishes a mythological vision of the creation of the American continent. It describes the original man and history in the virginal spaces of pristine America, before the arrival of the Spaniards. "La lámpara en la tierra" begins with a historical dialectic that will dominate the ideology of the canto:

> Antes de la peluca y la casaca
> fueron los ríos, ríos arteriales:
> fueron las cordilleras en cuya onda raída
> el condor o la nieve parecían inmóviles.
>
> (Before the wig and the cassock
> were the arterial rivers:
> were the mountains in whose torn waves
> the condor and the snow seemed frozen.)
> ("Amor América" [Love America], p. 7)

The wig and cassock, referring to the dress of the Spaniards who came to the New World, are a symbol of the new social order imposed. Before, America was a free and nameless territory, "Sin nombre todavía las pampas planetarias" (The planetary plains are yet nameless) ("Amor América," p. 7), which implies that the mission of the poet is to endow names, to impose meaning through language on a territory as yet unclaimed. In pronouncing that name in the poetic text, Neruda refutes the official historical versions and, at the same time, searches for its true identity.

Let us note that the line "El hombre tierra fue" (Man was earth) alludes to the ancestral state and the Biblical story of the creation of man from clay. Again like the Bible, *Canto general* opens with the concept of genesis and awakening. In this section, Neruda uses parallel verse constructions similar to those used in the Old Testament and in the Song of Songs.

Through alliterations and enumerations Neruda creates the feeling of entering the South American landscape, where we meet exotic animals and birds. Condors flying above the Andes and phosphorescent jaguars are described, creating a somnambulant tone that implies that the poet is a part of the very creation he is describing. After the animal kingdom, we are introduced to the land and the rivers: the Orinoco, Amazon, and Bío Bío. The reader travels over the most fecund lands as well as the most arid deserts, back to a genesis without theological origin.

After this rhythmic, sonorous structure that forms the basic matrix of the poem, Neruda introduces man, the Araucanian, who also emerged, like Adam, from clay:

> Como la copa de la arcilla era
> la raza mineral, el hombre
> hecho de piedras y de atmósfera
> limpio como los cántaros, sonoro.
>
> (Like the chalice of clay was
> the mineral race, man
> made of stones and atmosphere
> clean and sonorous like pitchers.)
> ("El hombre" [The man], p. 18)

The inhabitants of America are described with the same characteristics and chromatic images as the earth: the men are the color of copper, and the women are metallic doves. In this way Neruda establishes the connection with these first inhabitants who are not alien to the land but are part of it. They are contrasted to the outsiders who use wigs and cassocks. No God is present, and that terrifying image of the Old Testament where God is all powerful is totally absent in this section. Man emerges from earth and is molded in it.

"La lámpara en la tierra" performs an introductory function with respect to the rest of *Canto general,* which shows that this poem, despite having been written over a long period of time, is a coherent and well-crafted unit.

The Heights of Macchu Picchu

The pre-Columbian genesis with the earth and men that emerge from it are the protagonists of the first section of the *Canto general.* In the second, and perhaps the most important section of the *Canto,* there is a change in the cast of characters. Now it is the poet, the lyrical speaker, who narrates from the perspective of his own emotion and from his own chaos. These sections constitute a founding voice of an American reality.

Several motifs predominate throughout this poem that alone could be a self-sufficient unit. From cantos 1 through 5 the lyrical I appears as a traveler or pilgrim who speaks of a past. According to the majority of critics, the awareness of this past is linked to all the earlier poetry of Neruda, especially the *Residence* cycle. The tone of these initial verses transports us back to a past recently traversed and then speaks of a new present:

> Del AIRE al AIRE, como una red vacía,
> iba yo entre las calles y la atmósfera, llegando
> y despidiendo,
> en el advenimiento del otoño la moneda extendida
> de las hojas, y entre la primavera y las espigas,
> Lo que el más grande amor, como un guante
> que cae nos entrega como una larga luna.

> (From AIR to AIR, like an empty net,
> dredging through streets and ambient atmosphere,
>   I came
> lavish, at autumn's coronation, with the leaves
> proffer of currency and- between spring and wheat
>   ears
> that which a boundless love, caught in a gauntlet
>   fall,
> grant us like a long-fingered moon.)[11]

The poet, trapped in a routine stay on earth where man simply exists, wanders about, directionless, amid "clothing and smoke." Then he once again asks rhetorical questions, as he did in the *Residences:*

> ¿Qué era el hombre? ¿En qué parte de su conversación abierta
> entre los almacenes y los silbidos, en cuál de sus movimientos metálicos
> vivía lo indestructible, lo imperecedero, la vida?

> (What was man? In what layer of his humdrum conversation,
> among his shops and sirens, in which of his metallic movements
> lived on imperishably the quality of life?)
>   (section 1, p. 8)

These questions serve as a preamble to one of the most significant sections of the *Canto general,* the meditations on death and temporality. The third section speaks of a "small death" that could mean dying slowly day by day:

> cada día una muerte pequeña, polvo
> gusano, lámpara
> que se apaga en el lodo del suburbio,
> una pequeña muerte de alas gruesas
> entraba en cada hombre como una corta lanza.

> (each day a little death: dust
> maggot, lamp
> drenched in the mire of suburbs,
> a little death with fat wings
> entered into each man like a short blade.)
>
> (section 2, p. 12)

After these five preambles to the description of the remote past, the poet, overcome by the meditation on death, and immersed in a journey of interior quest, ascends to the lost city of Macchu Picchu, in the forgotten jungles of a vanished civilization. But this culture also was annihilated and had its own death, not the personal one described in stanzas one to five, not the death of the city, but "true death," that which annihilates an entire people.

Here we have the essential juxtaposition established in *The Heights of Macchu Picchu,* configurated by two movements, the descent toward the individual conscience of a past and the ascent toward the future:

> Entonces en la escala de la tierra he subido
> entre la atroz maraña de las selvas perdidas
> hasta tí, Macchu Picchu.

> (Then up the ladder of the earth I climbed
> through the barbed jungle thickets
> until I reached you, Macchu Picchu.)
>
> (section 6, p. 26)

In this ascent to the pre-Columbian citadel the poet reaches the culminating moment of the poem. In the ruins of a lost city, on the threshold of a sleeping past, the poet outlines with great clarity what has been enunciated in the previous five cantos: the "small death" that alluded to the social conventions of every day and the other death that cuts us off from our history and our past. The death of a people gives him the courage to regenerate himself in the "spent human spring" and to speak for all men.

The poet knows instinctively that the transcendence of one's own death is reached through others, through the history of those men buried and rediscovered in Macchu Picchu. That life among the stones was interrupted for a while and over it another history arose. Those who, like the ancient Egyptians, sculpted these stones and built this city were plain men, the makers of the true history of America:

> Mírame desde el fondo de la tierra,
> labrador, tejedor, pastor callado
>
> (Look at me from the depths of the earth
> tiller of fields, weaver, reticent shepherd)
>   (section 12, p. 66)

Paradoxically, it is a dead city, in ashes and ruins, a city of the past, that Neruda uses to tell the history of America and of his own self.

The idea of brotherhood is established when the lyrical speaker addresses "tú, hombre" and "tú, lector" ("you, man" and "you, reader") inviting us all to climb that path that he himself took when a mysterious prophetic voice bade him ascend. In this union with other men who lived in these ruins, the life of the poet and the life of those who could not speak or tell the past are permanently merged.

In section 7 the lyrical speaker proclaims the mission already established in the first canto of "La lámpara en la tierra." He wishes to hear the secret voices of those who cannot speak. Neruda, then, speaks to the dead in their tombs, a call that in poem 12 is made more explicit: "Mostrádme vuestra sangre y vuestro surco. Decidme aquí fui castigado" ("Show me your blood and your furrow. Say to me here I was scourged") (section 12, p. 67). His words resonate not only with the literary tradition of mythological voyages to the underworld but with Dante's *Inferno*.

The last stanza of *The Heights of Macchu Picchu* is a synthesis of the entire poem. The poet, now at one with a geographical space, raises his voice to vindicate his past and his present:

Dadme el silencio, el agua, la esperanza.
Dadme la lucha, el hierro, los volcanes.
Apegadme los cuerpos como imanes.
Acudid a mis venas y a mi boca.
Hablad por mis palabras y mi sangre.

(And give me silence, give me water, hope.
Give me the struggle, the irons, the volcanoes.
Let bodies cling like magnets to my body.
Come quickly to my veins and to my mouth.
Speak through my speech and through my blood.)
(section 12, p. 70)

The line "Speak through my words and my blood" brings to a close the journey of the pilgrim lost within himself.

The Heights of Macchu Picchu is a poem that represents a transnational American cultural identity that is a turning point in Neruda's artistic and political career. The poem was composed in 1945, two years after Neruda's visit to Macchu Picchu, an indication that the poem was the fruit of prolonged meditation.

The third canto, "Los conquistadores" (The conquerers), presents the arrival of the Spaniards in the New World. Neruda sees them as agents of evil and presents them in a consistently negative form. The fourth canto, entitled "Los libertadores" (The liberators), speaks of those who dedicated their lives to the struggle for the freedom of America. In this canto we find key figures of the history of Chile: the valiant Araucanians, Caupolicán, Lautaro, and more contemporary figures such as San Martín, Lincoln, and Sandino. The canto to the liberators ends with a hopeful poem in which the vital elements of fertility appear.

This section, the longest of the book, presents a wide range of themes that are repeated throughout *Canto general*. Neruda reiterates a one-sided version of the conquest, mentioning no positive aspect of the entire colonial period, the history of Chile, and its heroes.

The symbol of the tree, so essential in the *Canto,* reappears as an image of proliferation, resistance, and fecundity. The descriptions of the north of Chile, with its deserts and saltpeter mines, are filled with beautiful lyrical images that convey the peculiar beauty of this desolate area.[12]

"La arena traicionada" (Sand betrayed) recapitulates the sequential history of the conquerors, the liberators, and those who violate the progressive libertarian ideals of independence. "La arena traicionada" presents fabulous caricatures of dictators, such as Dr. Francia and García Moreno, and of the companies that exploited Latin America's riches, such as the United Fruit Company and Standard Oil. The deformed and monstruous descriptions of the Latin American dictators, almost caricatures, are particularly interesting. García Moreno, for example, is compared to a vicious jackal, and other tyrants are compared to various lowly and predatory forms of life. In the poem "La crema" (Cream) we find a synthesis of this parade of marauding animals and plants:

> apuestos tigres de Embajada
> pálidas niñas principales
> flores carnívoras, cultivos
> de las cavernas perfumadas,
> enredaderas chupadoras
> de sangre estiércol y sudor,
> lianas estranguladoras,
> cadenas de boas feudales.

> (elegant Embassy tigers
> pale prima donnas
> carnivorous flowers, plants
> from perfumed caverns,
> devouring vines
> of blood, manure and sweat,
> strangulating ivy,
> chains of feudal boas.)
>   ("La crema," Brugera ed., p. 171)

Though this section, "La arena traicionada," is one of the least studied of the *Canto general,* it is particularly important because of the vigorous language with which the poet describes the oppressing forces, creating for them a new mythology taken from the natural kingdom.

In the poem "Anaconda," Neruda speaks of the oligarchs who exploit miners in the Anaconda Copper Company. The title takes on increasing vitality in the book as Neruda links the figure of the anaconda serpent to the qualities of those associated with Anaconda as a company.[13]

The section ends with a poem dedicated to González Videla who adjudicated Neruda's expulsion order, thus beginning the exile in which the long poem "El fugitivo" (The fugitive) was written.

Section seven, the shortest of the collection, has two themes: a recapitulation of the earlier sections where the American space is described and a return to the rewriting of history from a new perspective.

The vision of nature in "América no invoco tu nombre en vano" (America, I do not invoke your name in vain) is conveyed through surrealistic images, sometimes apparently unconnected and dispersed. There are poems of a strong dreamlike visionary quality, and the language is charged with implicit social content as well.

The final poem of this section takes up the same theme sketched in *The Heights of Macchu Picchu:* the hope of peoples for freedom and autonomy. In this canto we see the reappearance of the motifs of light, morning, and awakening. The fact that America's name will not be written in vain synthesizes the message of the chronicler from the beginning of the canto through part 7, and it seals the two very important configurations of the book, which are the poetic history of the continent and Neruda's own personal history. The poet appears as chronicler and as voice of other men, especially those who are speechless. *Canto general* is an incitation to awaken those men fallen outside of history.

It is easy to establish the relationship between the "Canto de América" and the "Canto de Chile." Neruda nostalgically describes the Chilean topography. He writes of an untouched land, fresh with flowers and pollen. In the poem "Eternidad" (Eternity) Neruda again returns to the childhood matrix and all the organic elements that form a part of his poetic vision: wood, rivers, and trees. In "Himno y regreso" (Hymn and return) Neruda speaks to the earth of its origins and of his own necessity to be embraced by it. Throughout the "Canto de Chile" Neruda praises the folk art traditions of his country: the weavers, the potters, and the basket makers. After describing the manual arts, Neruda transports us to the desolated desert of Atacama and to the hard lives of the miners, completing the portrait of his country from south to north.

Following the "Canto de Chile" is "La tierra se llama Juan" (The earth is called Juan) in which language is stripped of all rhetoric, as Neruda himself said in interviews, so that everyone can understand. This idea is made explicit in the section "Yo soy" (I am) where he says:

> No escribo para que otros libros me aprisionen
> ni para encarnizados aprendices de lirio,
> sino para sencillos habitantes que piden
> agua y luna, elementos del orden inmutable
> escuelas, pan, vino, guitarras y herramientas.
> Escribo para el pueblo, aunque no pueda
> leer mi poesía con sus ojos rurales.

> (I do not write so that other books can imprison me,
> nor for the avid apprentices of lilies,
> I write for humble people that ask for
> water and moon, elements of immutable order
> schools, bread, wine guitars and tools.
> I write for the people though they
> may not be able to read my poetry with their rural eyes.)
>   ("Yo soy," section 20, Brugera ed., p. 430)

In this section the poems are narrated in the simulated voice of the people themselves, which gives the poem greater efficacy and veracity. The historical descriptions seem totally authentic. Neruda also describes the suffering of working people, especially the mine workers, and speaks of their marginal position in society. In this section, as in *Heights of Macchu Picchu*, hope and the possibility of change stand out. Neruda makes clear that behind all the glorious liberators are the invisible men, the "Juanes" of every day:

> Juan, es tuya la puerta y el camino
> la tierra
> es tuya pueblo, la verdad ha nacido
> contigo, de tu sangre.
> No pudieron exterminarte. . . .

> (Juan, the door and the road
> are yours
> yours, People, the truth is born
> with you, in your blood
> they could not exterminate you.)
>   ("La tierra se llama Juan," section 17,
>   Brugera ed., p. 269)

"Que despierte el leñador" (Let the woodcutter awaken) follows closely the idea of "La tierra se llama Juan," since in it Neruda speaks of the North American man, the common man who is exploited, like his Latin American brother, by the policies of multinational corporations. This section represents an invocation and, also, a petition to the Colossus of the North for world peace. The figure of Abraham Lincoln is invoked as a mythified hero of the Americas. The veracity that emanates from all these voices that silently shaped history contributes to the testimonial nature of the *Canto.*

"El fugitivo" contains an autobiographical section on the life of the poet who narrates his dramatic experiences when he was forced to seek refuge in the homes of Chilean people throughout the country, at the time of the detention order issued by González Videla. The recurring symbols of this canto are the night and the darkness, so expressive of the sadness of this episode in his life. Nonetheless, "El fugitivo" is also a collective history, the history of a strike in the gold mines of the desolated and difficult terrain of northern Chile. Here again Neruda reiterates the sentiments of *The Heights of Macchu Picchu,* the importance of being the chronicler of the history of his people.

"Los ríos del canto" (The rivers of song) is a reflection on friendship, war, and creation. Of special interest is the poem dedicated to the Spanish poet Miguel Hernández, a shepherd poet of Castille who died as a prisoner after the Civil War. Neruda pays lyrical tribute to a man who taught with his life and triumphed over death through his poetry.

"El genésis oceánico" (The great ocean) postulates the genesis of the ocean, just as "La lámpara en la tierra" did with the earth. We find the same amalgam of mythopoetic images that appeared in the metaphorical creation of the earth genesis in the first section. "El genésis oceánico" is a seminal, transforming canto in which we perceive the poet's own fabulation of the ocean's creation."[14]

"El genésis oceánico" consists of twenty-four sections evocative of the world's beginnings, described with an almost cosmic energy. The remaining sections speak of the emergence of man, the sea, and the objects that live in it. Neruda also sings to the great ocean surrounding the mysterious Rapa Nui, Easter Island. Neruda establishes the same connection between the pre-Columbian past and the navigator who visits these sites in the twentieth century that he made between Incas and contemporary visitors in *The Heights of Macchu Picchu.*

Some observations can be made regarding the structure of the major section of the *Canto* within the totality of the poem. There are three equidistant cantos: "La lámpara en la tierra," "Canto de Chile," and "El genésis oceánico," which take the following numeration: one, seven, and fourteen.

The *Canto general* closes with an autobiographical section entitled "Yo soy" (I am), but here it is not an individual "I" but the sum of the experience of the people and the poet. Thus the book reorders itself around its starting point.

At first the encyclopedic character of *Canto general* will cause the reader, confronted with such an abundance of images, sensations, and history, some confusion. A careful reading, however, shows the *Canto* to be a meticulously crafted book. The visit to the lost city of Macchu Picchu centers the book around the basic concept of the identification with America's roots. In the *Canto general*, Latin America and Neruda's spiritual commitment to it appear as a fully developed poetic creed. [15]

Chapter Five
Memorial de Isla Negra, Memoirs: A Journey of Introspection

The *Memorias: Confieso que he vivido (Memoirs),* [1] published for the first time in 1974, constitutes an illuminating picture of the poet's personality. To read these intensely lyrical evocations and descriptions is to realize that poetry permeates everything that Neruda wrote, including the prose. The *Memoirs* explains the development of Neruda's poetry so that the reader can familiarize himself with the motivation behind certain poems.

The *Memoirs* was written for Brazilian newspaper *O Cruzeiro Internazional,* in 1962. Ten years later, in the solitude and tranquillity of Isla Negra, Neruda decided to develop these columns into the story of his life. He continued to work on the *Memoirs* up until the last days of his life, which tragically coincided with the military takeover of the government of Chile and the death of his dear friend Salvador Allende.

The collection consists of twelve intensely personal, lyrical notebooks, filled with the poetic flights so characteristic of Neruda. He himself makes a careful distinction between autobiographical memories, concerned with facts and details, and poetic impressions, which are concentrated on epiphanies.

The *Memoirs* describes with intimate detail marvelous scenes of Neruda's childhood and his adventures in the mountains in the company of his father, the train engineer. As in all of Neruda's work, there are constant descriptions of the Chilean countryside and forests: "Bajo los volcanes, junto a los ventisqueros, entre los grandes lagos, el fragante, el silencioso, el enmarañado bosque chileno . . ." (Under the volcanoes, beside the snow-capped mountains, among the huge lakes, the fragrant, the silent, the tangled Chilean forest . . .") (*Memoirs,* p. 5).

It is a metaphorical passage whose powerful language creates a palpable and realistic picture of the Chilean forest. The colorful ensemble of adjectives and images evokes the natural surroundings with an almost visceral feeling.

Along with these lyrical descriptions of nature, Neruda reveals narrative gifts. In the essay entitled "The House of the Three Widows" he tells of once hiking through the woods and becoming lost. He arrived at a mysterious house inhabited by three French ladies who still served their table with all the gentility of the aristocratic French tradition.

The *Memoirs* proceeds according to chronological history, yet it is not bound by dates. Each notebook corresponds approximately to a book of poetry. When Neruda speaks of his youth and the sunsets he contemplated in Santiago, or the boarding house he lived in, or the friends who influenced him, we have the context of *Crepusculario* and *Twenty Love Poems.*

He recalls a dear friend, Alberto Rojas Jiménez, whose premature death is commemorated in a poem in the *Residence.* Neruda remembers the youthful passions that inspired him and registers his consternation on learning that a young student had taken his own life after reading *Residence on Earth.*

The notebook, *The Roads of the World,* dedicated to the Far East, allows us to understand the alienation the poet experienced in those countries. Neruda takes us to places like Colombo, Ceylon, and Batavia. We discover the anecdotal experiences behind such key moments in his poetic work as the "Widower's Tango," found in the first *Residence,* dedicated to the volatile and jealous Josie Bliss. In the notebook fragment that bears her name as title, Neruda remembers her with melancholy as a ghost who never ceases to pursue him. The farewell scene where Josie kisses the poet's shoes and departs is especially memorable. The knowledge of these experiences permits the reader to enter into complicity with the writer.

The notebooks in which Neruda speaks in the most passionate terms are those dedicated to Spain and Federico Garcia Lorca. He re-creates Lorca's joyful personality and his tragic assassination by Falangist forces in Granada. Neruda also pays homage to other outstanding figures of Spanish-language poetry, such as César Vallejo, Gabriela Mistral, Vicente Huidobro, and such novelists of the "Boom" as Gabriel García Marquez, José Donoso, and Julio Cortázar.

In addition to the praise and affection expressed for his fellow writers, he mentions the controversy about his fame and the criticism of which he was the object because of his eventual prosperity. Here Neruda defends himself admirably, saying that every poet has the right to live honorably from his craft and that all artists deserve to enjoy material well-being. Nowhere do we find Neruda expressing either bitterness or resentment. The only anger is that expressed in the last pages of the *Memoirs* when Neruda speaks of his friend Allende, gunned down in the presidential palace during the 1973 coup. He finishes the *Memoirs,* just days before his own death, with a desolating phrase about the betrayal of Chile by Chileans and a dramatic account of the last days of the coup. The figure of Allende's destroyed body foreshadows many other bodies to fall in Chile. The tone of this passage becomes tense and tragic. Neruda, despite his terminal illness, never ceased to participate in the events of his country, which indicates to what extent Chile and its history form the basis of his poetry.

The *Memoirs* is virtually the only primary source for understanding Neruda's concept of poetry. The notebook entitled *Poetry is a Craft* declares poetry to be the property of plain people, transcending all social barriers. This indicates that Neruda recognizes the self-absorption of the *Residences.* In the *Memoirs,* poetry is likened to a wooden object, painstakingly crafted by the poet-artisan. Neruda is impatient with theoreticians of poetry (or of politics or sex, for that matter). Pablo Neruda is more artisan than aesthete. He defines poetry as that which is rendered poetic. As an artisan, Neruda compares poetry to a loaf of bread, or a ceramic plate, or a sculpted piece of wood. Action, not theory, is the road chosen by the poet. He believes in the mutual understanding of poet and people, the invisible audience. Poetry must communicate through the most universal of themes—nature and love. It is an altruistic, civic act. For this reason, in the introduction to the memoirs, Neruda says "My life is a life made up of many lives."

In a number of instances in this text, under the heading "Poetry Is an Occupation," two apparently contradictory words, "reason" and "inspiration," are used in a coherent logical combination. He admits that in his young days he was mistaken in believing that one should trust inspiration and now takes reason, too, as a guide. Reason acts as a moderating force that helps the poet search for concentration and balance within the creative process, an act often considered beyond reason. The poet appears to use the word "reason" to denote the senses, to mean a critical capacity to discriminate and to choose the representative dimension of language.

The notion of communication is another aspect to be emphasized within Neruda's poetics. Neruda considers poetry an ennobling force and an act of love that dignifies man. The political function completes his concept of poetry. The closeness of the poet to his people is not divorced from the aesthetic search for language. Thus Neruda seeks the modes of expression used in conversational language as his means of communication.

Beginning with *Canto general*, particularly the section entitled "El fugitivo" in which Neruda narrates his own experience as exile from the Ibañez regime, the autobiographical element stands out as a fundamental part of his lyrical production. In *Isla Negra: A Notebook*, too, he uses the autobiographical convention. The *Memoirs* may be seen as the culmination of this process in verse now cast in a highly lyrical prose.

Para nacer he nacido

There is a companion volume to the *Memoirs, Para nacer he nacido,* translated by Margaret Sayers Peden as *Passions and Impressions* (1981), which is a selection of prose compositions compiled by Matilde Urrutia and the Venezuelan novelist Miguel Otero Silva.[2] This volume contains the youthful work of Neruda published in the University of Chile newspaper *Claridad.* Texts such as "Yo acuso" ("I accuse"), from the period of political persecutions in Chile under González Videla, and the Nobel acceptance speech are included.

All of these writings, collected in one volume, allow us to appreciate Neruda's narrative gifts. He recounts his personal encounters with Chilean and foreign mentors and describes authors such as the novelists Mariano Latorre and Pedro Prado. Also in this book we find colorful descriptions of the open-air markets of the Orient and Mexico, with their exhibits of artisanry. In "Poetas de los pueblos" ("Poets of the Peoples"), Neruda repeats the concept that South America is a land of artisans and of popular poets. These declarations facilitate our understanding of his play about the popular nineteenth-century hero, Joaquín Murieta, who is a figure of Latin American folklore. Neruda speaks of the artisanry of Chile, especially the naive embroideries from Isla Negra, which he later took to the Louvre to be exhibited.

The *Memoirs* and its sequels offer the reader and the critic an insight into Neruda's private self. Many threads—friends who influenced the poet, women whom he loved, and reflections on his craft—merge in the *Memoirs.* The poet speaks little about his favorite books and authors—this is a closely guarded secret from which he apparently wishes to exclude us. The most curious omission is the name of Nicanor Parra, colleague and sometime literary antagonist. Neither does he mention Nicanor's sister Violeta, or most curious of all, María Luisa Bombal, the distinguished novelist with whom Neruda lived in Buenos Aires during his time as Chilean consul there.

Memorial de Isla Negra

Isla Negra: A Notebook is a series of five books published in the 1960s. *Isla Negra* is less autobiographical and anecdotal than the *Memoirs.* It represents the personal vision of a poet who at the age of sixty dedicates himself to exploring the course his poetry has taken.

Unlike the *Memoirs,* with their chronologically ordered notebooks, the *Isla Negra* follows a quasi-historical sequence in which the poet presents a vision from his own imagination. Thus the autobiography becomes a testimony in which the real and the fictitious are joined, inducing the reader to discover for himself how the creator saw and ordered the events of his own life. The poet's memory is intermittent and indeterminate and ranges over the full extent of his experiences. In a sense the English title *Isla Negra: A Notebook* conveys better than the Spanish the quality of the book.[3]

The narrative "I" frequently omits such personal issues as the death of Neruda's only daughter, revealing that the version presented is controlled and premeditated.

The five books of *Isla Negra* consist of a sequence of five unities or lyrical spaces written in the form of a notebook. The translator and literary critic Ben Bellit has written that these books represent a lyrical odyssey through the four elements of nature, which act accordingly "as a unifying module." Bellit says that water represents the rainy childhood of the south of Chile and that air is the implicit erotic element, fire the revolutionary spirit, and earth the return of

Neruda to his roots. With the last book of the collection, *Sonata crítica (Critical Sonata)*, this cosmology disappears.[4]

Isla Negra: A Notebook represents the view of the traveler who returns to ancestral roots not to contemplate himself but to discover who he was. The book projects a kaleidoscopic and cinematographic vision that lingers like a painter's brush on certain leitmotivs of his poetics.

Donde nace la lluvia (Where the Rain is Born) with its suggestive water imagery, so crucial to the Nerudian cosmovison, is the first book of the collection and the most autobiographical. It covers the period from 1904–21, that is, from the birth of the poet in Parral until his arrival in Santiago. The collection closes with the poem "Los crepúsculos de Maruri" ("Sunsets of Maruri"). He reveals in these poems the stages of childhood and adolescence as he experienced them in Temuco: "Nascimiento" ("The Birth"), "La mamadre" ("The More-Mother"), and "El padre" ("The Father"). In "The Birth" we find the retrospective vision of things that have vanished, eroded by the powers of nature and time, the house and the streets destroyed by an earthquake. The themes of nature and time take on a singular importance, as they do in the posthumous poetry, because poet tries to recover them through deceptive memory: "Yo no tengo memoria / del paisaje ni del tiempo" ("I have no memory / of landscape or time") ("The Birth," p.5).

Neruda seeks to conjure up the mother he never saw, but there is no response except silence and shadow from the regions of death. The last verse is a description of place he associates with the image of the mother:

> Parral de tierra temblorosa,
> tierra cargada de uvas
> que nacieron
> desde mi madre muerta.
>
> (Parral of the trembling earth,
> a land laden with grapes
> which came to life
> out of my dead mother.)
>   ("The Birth," p. 6)

The image of the earth and the mother enfolded in it are identified as creative forces, as if the mother were a root giving life to the vines and their grapes. Neruda unifies the disintegration of the childhood space and the creation of a new life through the image of the mother.

Along with this poem to the mother whom the poet never knew, is one dedicated to "La mamadre" whom the young Neftali Reyes adored. He describes her like a magical substance in his life, a woman who measures flour, launders, irons, and cures him of fevers. This evocation is much more tangible than the one in "Nascimiento" and contrasts markedly with the image of woman in earlier works.

In the poem entitled "El sexo" ("Sex") Neruda narrates his first sexual experiences, associating femininity with bread and warmth, similar to the description of "La mamadre." Bread appears thoughout Neruda's poetry in the form of wheat fields in *Twenty Love Poems,* or in the magic of domestic order in *One Hundred Love Sonnets,* and also as a religious image: bread, linked to the female and the earth essence, signifies regeneration.

Among the poems dedicated to childhood is one called "The Father." The father appeared in *Canto general* as a rather remote figure in the personal life of the poet. Here Neruda's vision is ambivalent and combines fear and admiration, as well as sadness for his father's hardships. The poem, which begins "Mi pobre padre duro / " ("My poor hard father / "), summarizes his attitude towards a man absorbed in his labor:

> Y entre su madrugar y sus caminos,
> entre llegar para salir corriendo,
> un día con más lluvia que otros días
> el conductor José del Carmen Reyes
> subió al tren de la muerte y hasta ahora no ha vuelto.

> (And between his early risings and his traveling,
> between arriving and rushing off,
> one day, rainier than any other days,
> the railwayman José del Carmen Reyes
> climbed aboard the train of death and so far has not come back.)
>   ("The Father," p. 12)

The poet presents the father in an equivocal light that indicates he hardly knew him. There are few details of intimacy, as opposed to what we find in the poem dedicated to "La mamadre." The poet captures the child's emotion when confronted with the powerful figure of the father. Neruda, the man, seems to comprehend what that child of yesterday felt seeing the father go off on interminable trips across mountain passes on his train. Perhaps this retrospective evocation, joined to the tenderness and the maturity of understanding, is the key to this first book of the *Isla Negra*.

The following verses from "Niño perdido" ("Little Boy Lost") exemplify the notion of time that passes and disintegrates not in tragic and disordered vision, but with resignation that we cannot recapture what was:

> Todo se fue mudando hoja por hoja
> en el árbol, ¿Y en ti? Cambió tu piel,
> tu pelo, tu memoria. Aquel no fuiste.
>
> (Everything kept changing leaf by leaf
> on the tree. And you? Your skin changed
> your hair, your memory. You were not that other one.)
>
> ("Little Boy Lost," p. 43)

Neruda uses a combination of verb tenses in these five books to create a union between present and past, as we see in the poem about the father, with its blending of the tones of past recollections and present realities.

The rain as a powerful force eroding at the same time that it nourishes buried loved ones, such as the *mamadre* and the father, is part of the water imagery so essential in this book of lyrical and autobiographical evocations where the poet begins his pilgrimage through the past. The poet bids farewell to Parral in the poem "El tren nocturno" ("Night Train") about the train that pulls him away from his beloved South.

"Night Train" exemplifies the introspective quality of *Isla Negra*, with its intense reliving of childhood and regret at losing the security of the maternal womb. The image of the train is meant to signify not only the movement from the provincial South but the arrival at an unfamiliar and ambivalent state of being. The poem begins with the description of a third-class train compartment filled with travelers in ponchos dampened with rain and mud. The lyrical speaker says:

> Oh largo Tren Nocturno,
> muchas veces
> desde el sur hacia el norte,
> entre ponchos mojados,
> cereales,
> botas tiesas de barro,
> en Tercera,
> fuiste desenrollando geografía.
> Tal vez comencé entonces
> la página terrestre,
> aprendí los kilómetros
> del humo
> la extensión del silencio.
>
> (The long night train,
> so often,
> south to north,
> with wet ponchos,
> grain,
> boots clogged with mud,
> in third class,
> you ran on, unwinding geography.
> Perhaps it was then I began
> my diary of the earth.
> I learned the kilometers
> of smoke
> the spread of silence.)
>   ("Night Train," p. 60)

Smoke and silence are the reiterated coordinates not only of *Isla Negra* but also of much of Neruda's poetry. The smoke alludes to the ineffability of experience, and the silence marks the passage of time. The poem continues with an extensive description of landmarks of the Chilean countryside and may be compared to the similar topographical references found in the "Canto de Chile" section of the *Canto general*. Neruda in the *Isla Negra*, uses a language of chromatic and tactile images that conjure up the intense sensual pleasures of childhood. In the "Canto de Chile" the images refer to mankind and its place in history, while the language of *Isla Negra* is wholly lyrical and personal. Once the topography and the image of the traveler are developed, a third component emerges—the reference to a former self now dissolved into memories. The images of greenery and light are replaced by others of urban indifference:

Algo me separaba de mi sangre
y al salir asustado
por la calle
supe, porque sangraba,
que me habían cortado las raíces

(Something was separating me from my blood
and, going out in shock to
the street,
I knew [because I was bleeding]
that my roots had been cut off.)
                                        ("Night Train," p. 64)

The journey is not that of a mythic hero searching for a new land, but one of loss and alienation from roots. Neruda never stops reliving the childhood so magically evoked in *Where the Rain is Born.*

La luna en el laberinto

The Moon in the Labyrinth covers the chronological period from 1919 to 1921, a period in which the young Neruda fully entered the literary life of the capital. *The Moon in the Labyrinth,* like *Where the Rain is Born,* continues in a chronological and historical sequence that is to some extent faithful to the poet's autobiography.

There are sequences of love poems dedicated to three different women, Teresa (a name that in Spanish is associated with earth, "tierra"), Rosaura, and Delia del Carril, his second wife. In his *Memoirs,* Neruda calls Teresa and Rosaura by the invented names of Marisol and Marisombra.

Teresa is the beloved of childhood and early adolescence in Temuco, and so her image appears associated with rain, wood, and the emanations of nature. She is of the fruitful earth source, the country woman fragrant of wood and rain, which recalls to us some of the poems dedicated to Matilde in *One Hundred Love Sonnets.*

Rosaura represents a counterpoint. She is the adolescent love of the city who appeared as the student of the gray beret in *Twenty Love Poems.* Though love is the only force of redemption, both lovers are described as impossible.

Neruda again recalls dear friends such as the beloved Alberto Rojas Jiménez, about whom he wrote two unforgettable elegies. We may compare the vision of Rojas Jiménez in the second *Residence,* where the friend appears as a magical being who flies and sings, with a demythified view of Jiménez here in *The Moon in the Labyrinth*.

There are poems like traveler's odysseys about Paris, Rangoon, and Ceylon, where the Orient seems a fateful continent of false idols, as false as the West: "Allí en Rangoon comprendí que los dioses / eran tan enemigos como Dios / del pobre ser humano" ("There in Rangoon I understood that the gods / were also enemies of the poor human being) ("Religion in the East," p.124). In these poems Neruda relives the cycle of the *Residences* and the solitude he felt in those latitudes.

Among the poems dedicated to the Orient we find "Rangoon 1927," which narrates an erotic adventure with a harlot. Another poem, "Aquellas vidas" ("Those Lives"), talks about a woman who burns herself at the bank of a river:

> Y si algo vi en mi vida fue una tarde
> en la India, en las márgenes de un río:
> arder una mujer de carne y hueso,
> y no sé si era el alma o era el humo
> lo que del sarcófago salía.
>
> (If I remember anything in my life
> it was an afternoon in India, on the banks of a river:
> They were burning a woman of flesh and bone.
> And I didn't know if it was soul or smoke
> that came from the sarcophagus.)
>   ("Those Lives," p.134)

This scene, which might seem gratuitous, takes on a special meaning in notebook 4 of the *Memoirs,* where Neruda tells in prose the true story of a girl in love who immolates herself beside a river. The woman aflame, transfigured in the poem, is revealed in the *Memoirs,* twenty years later, as a real woman. This incident never ceased to haunt the poet.

The collection closes with an introspective poem that bespeaks the security of the poet in his present existence. He no longer belongs to his past, yet he is still the man who lived those lives now seen as alien and distant:

> Porque de tantas vidas que tuve estoy ausente
> Y soy, a la vez soy aquel hombre que fui.

(Because in many lives I am absent.
I am here now and I am also the man I was,
both at the same time.)
("No hay pura luz" ["There Is No Clear Light"], p. 147)

The title of this collection is based on two metaphors: the labyrinth of city life and solitude and the moon, which illuminates the labyrinth where the poet wanders and seeks the path of poetry.

El fuego cruel

Cruel Fire, the third book of Isla Negra, is thematically related to the Spanish Civil War, but the chronology is not synchronized with autobiography. For example, we find poems about the Orient that logically belong to The Moon in the Labyrinth. But this somewhat chaotic ordering of the collection emphasizes that it grew in response to the unfolding of the poet's imagination. In the two poems dedicated to Josie Bliss, the violent and jealous Burmese woman, she becomes a phantasmagoric memory, arriving like a specter to stir the poet's sense of guilt for abandoning her:

Josie Bliss me alcanzó revolviendo
mi amor y su martirio
¡Lanzas de ayer, espadas del pasado!
Soy culpable, le dije
a la luciérnaga,
Y me envolvío la noche.

(Josie Bliss caught up with me, upsetting
my love and her martyrdom.
Spears of yesterday, swords of the past!
I am guilty, I said
to the firefly.
And the night enveloped me.)
("Amores Josie Bliss" ["Loves Josie Bliss"], p.200)

The intriguing figure of Josie Bliss appears sporadically in Neruda's poetry and in the Memoirs as well, where he recalls her as the jealous lover who stalked him, dressed in white and knife in hand. Sara Vial's biography of Neruda in Valparaíso speaks of Josie Bliss as a wild, eternal, even menacing presence that constantly haunts Neruda. Josie is also a treasure trove of poetic material for Neruda.

The poem "Loves Josie Bliss II" shows the synthesis of dispersed elements linked to the history of this woman in Neruda's life:

> Tus ojos aguerridos,
> tus pies desnudos
> dibujando un rayo,
> tu rencor de puñal, tu beso duro
> como los frutos del desfiladero,
> ayer, ayer,
> viviendo en el ruido del fuego.
>
> (Your embattled eyes,
> your bare feet
> tracing a sunray,
> your dagger anger, your hard kiss
> like fruits of the ravine
> yesterday, yesterday
> living on the crackle of fire.)
>   ("Loves Josie Bliss," p.208)

These verses present a physical description of the Burmese woman, fluctuating between fury (the poet calls her "furia mía") and the regret for an abandoned and helpless woman. The description centers on violent eyes and nude feet, a cipher for savage primitivism and also purity. The images of nude feet, lightning, and sword all create a ghostly picture of a woman's rancor and uncontrolled passion.

This lengthy poem written in free verse reflects the demented flavor of the *Residences.* This poem is an excellent opportunity to observe the poet registering visions of the past and dealing with a real phenomenon.

The poems dictated to Josie Bliss, such as the "Widow's Tango," can be compared to those in the second *Residence* where the poet turns his gaze to the woman who inspired his poem and tries to throw off her influence and to think of her as dead: "Y ya no pueden buscarme tus caderas extinguidas" ("Now I cannot be pursued by your extinguished hips") ("Loves Josie Bliss," p. 208).

In the same collection are poems related to the concept of the poet as witness of historical events such as the Spanish Civil War, the dictatorship of González Videla, and the political awakening of the working class in Chile. The poet affirms that he is returning to his country with new eyes and a socal commitment.

A new element is the description of the poet entering the dwellings of the miners and how this experience made his poetry change
direction. He insists on the term "testimony"—bearing witness,
affirming, speaking out. The essentially political poems of *Cruel
Fire* and the *Memoirs* of Neruda express the same immovable
convictions.

In *Cruel Fire* we find a number of poems dedicated to the poet's
exile both inside and outside of the country. Those dedicated to his
inner exile, in which Neruda speaks of the people who protected
him and gave him refuge, are essential to an understanding of this
period of absolute transformation in the political ideology of Neruda.
Exile is a nightmare attenuated by the men who sheltered him. In
the poem "Revoluciones" ("Revolutions"), the poet indicates that
through suffering the human being grows to understand the meaning
of brotherhood and the human family.

As we said earlier, *Cruel Fire* has a social and political focus that
begins with the warm reminiscences of prewar Madrid, that city so
beloved but now haunted by death. Then the book takes on an
ascending and climactic shape when the social struggle emerges as
an instrument of social change.

In one of the final poems, "Parthenón" ("Parthenon"), which
connotes order and perfection, the poet indicates the hope for a
harmonious future where man returns to state of civility, through
the redemptive force of love:

> Estoy seguro
> de la piedra inmóvil,
> pero conozco el viento.
> El orden es sólo una criatura.
> Crece y vuelve a vivir el edificio.
> Una vez y otra vez se apaga el fuego,
> pero vuelve el amor a su morada.
>
> (I am sure of
> the motionless stone
> but I know the wind.
> Order is just a creature.
> It grows and the building comes back to life.
> At one time or another, the fire goes out
> but love returns to its dwelling place.
> ("Parthenon," p. 224)

Cruel Fire is perhaps Neruda's closest approximation to biographical and poetic historicity, beginning with the reminiscences of the Spanish Civil War and continuing through the poet's expatriation during the González Videla government. The poems also contain, as promised in the title, a significant double connotation that has repercussions throughout the collection: fire as a malignant and cruel force as well as fire in the Promethean sense of a gift. Thanks to the struggle within the conscience of the poet, the destiny of the dispossessed is vindicated:

> y era mi poesía la bandera
> sobre
> tantas congojas,
> la que desde el navío los llamaba
> latiendo y acogiendo
> los legados
> de la descubridora
> desdichada,
> de la madre remota que me otorgó la sangre y la palabra.

> (and my poetry was the flag
> that flew over
> so much anguish
> that summoned them from the ship
> waving and welcoming,
> legacy
> of the unfortunate
> discoverer,
> the remote mother
> who gave me blood and voice.)
>   ("Misión de amor" ["Mission of Love"], p. 162)

El cazador de raíces

The Hunter of Roots, rather than autobiography, is an analysis of the present. As Rodríguez Monegal points out in *El viajero inmóvil,* Neruda is in a period of self-contemplation. Though there are references to the past, there is a greater attachment to the present than ever before. The first poem exposes the predominant theme of the book, the preoccupation with death and the search for immortality.

The long poem "Cita de invierno" ("Appointment with Winter") alludes to the fact that the poet finds himself awaiting his own death, while other men anticipate happiness and companionship. The entire poem is suffused with a melancholic and elegiac tone. Despite solitude and lack of communication with other men, the poet has not lost contact with the roots he constantly seeks. "Appointment with Winter" is a powerfully introspective poem in which the poet refers to the many changes that have shaped his life. Like grains of sand pouring through an hour glass, he says, his face has disappeared in time.

In the poem "Bosque" ("Forest") the earth is perceived as being in a constant state of regeneration. The earth resuscitates dead substances; putrefaction nourishes other roots and gives life. The poet longs for a profound identification with the telluric archetype inherent in the forest, but now the idea of his origin expands and is no longer solely Parral or the deceased mother, but is a search for a more universal entity. The roots are the means of attaining metaphysical union between man and his surroundings. The idea of immortality is also associated with the idea of earth and roots as part of the search for integration.

The poet's creative food is the root and origin, which symbolizes the dialectics of life and death. As the earth nourishes itself on dead substances in order to give life, death is an affirmation of existence:

> Calla la tierra para que no sepan
> sus nombres diferentes, ni su extendido idioma,
> calla porque trabaja
> recibiendo y naciendo:
> cuanto muere recoge
> como una anciana hambrienta:
>
> (The earth is mute so as not to reveal
> its different names or its vast language.
> It is mute because it works away,
> taking in, giving birth.
> Whatever dies, it gathers in
> like an ancient hungry creature.)
> ("El cazador en el bosque" ["The Hunter in the Forest"],
> p. 239)

This vision of the life-death dialectic is radically different from the vision of final disintegration that appeared in the *Residences*. Now the mature poet becomes a philosopher. Although death does exist, it is not definitive because from a tree of dead roots other substances find nourishment. To survive, the poet must attach himself to that same root. In *El cazador de raíces* he makes an almost ecological statement: man, to exist, must cohabit with the earth.

The resurrection of being, in a nonbiological sense, is the object of Neruda's search in this book. *The Hunter of Roots* departs from the Judeo-Christian separation of life and death and allies itself to the primitive doctrines where earth and the perishable, united and resurrected, return to the essence that originally gave life.

But despite fame and wealth, Neruda feels persecuted, hated, and attacked. He alludes to being a "masked poet" who must protect himself. He uses the concept of the astute hunter, as one who seeks the roots of belonging and also to shield himself from those who stalk him. Despite the fact that the poet recognizes envy and hatred, he continues to be benevolent towards his enemies and to love them. As he says, "Los amé cuanto pude, en su desdicha" ("I loved them as much as I could, in their misfortune") ("Para la envidia," "To Envy," p. 309).

Neruda indicates that he is not in harmony with his fellow men and that he prefers solitude. He chooses silence to protect himself from the envy of others and to escape, seeking not the communion of *Canto general* or the *Odes,* but the harmony of the natural cycles.

Neruda finds himself paradoxically far from men and seeks refuge within the only possible space the poet can inhabit: himself:

> Vengo a buscar raíces,
> las que hallaron
> el alimento mineral del bosque,
> la substancia
> tenaz, el cinc sombrío
> el cobre venenoso.
>
> Esa raiz debe nutrir mi sangre.
>
> (I come to look for my roots,
> the ones that discovered,
> the mineral food of the forest,
> that fierce substance,
> gloomy zinc,
> poisonous copper.
>
> that root has to nourish my blood.)
> (The Hunter in the Forest," p. 240)

Sonata crítica (1964)

Sonata crítica (Critical Sonata) differs from the previous four books in certain essential ways. The autobiographical element diminishes and the poet centers his reflections on the present and his disappointment with his fellow men, expressing his doubts and reservations. Many poems allude to the fact that the poet, because of his visionary gifts, is permanently separated from other men.

The predominant themes in these poems are the mission of art, the role of the poet, and the poet's relations with others. The first poem, "Arte magnética" ("Magnetic Art"), indicates the belief that the poet is a wanderer, constantly in search of the telluric matrix that permits him to create. This poem introduces the principal theme of the collection: that solitude is felt most acutely in the presence of others.

"Los desavenidos" ("To Those at Odds") and "Las comunicaciones" ("The Communications") speak of shattered matrimonial relations and the wish for a more authentic male-female communication. The world now seems to be a battle ground of warring couples, as Neruda abandons his earlier idealization of love and addresses the very modern theme of lack of communication. Life is seen as a card game. Later the poet wonders how he can possibly participate in this tangle of human chaos:

> Que alguien mire y me diga,
> mire el juego del tiempo,
> las horas de la vida,
> las cartas del silencio,
> la sombra y sus designios,
> y me diga que juego
> para seguir perdiendo.
>
> (Someone look and tell me,
> look at the game of time,
> the hours of our life,
> the playing cards of silence,
> the shadow and its purpose,
> and tell me what to play
> to keep on losing.)
>
> ("A la baraja" ["To the Pack"], p. 329)

These poems postulate an ethic of what human behavior should be. They are filled with question marks and are written in a sarcastic, sardonic tone. The poet finds no exit from his social alienation. At a loss to explain the disintegration of the sense of community, he can only wonder how he will find the road back:

> Dónde está la verdad? Pero la llave
> se extravió en un ejército de puertas
> y allí está entre las otras,
> sin hallar
>   nunca más
>   su cerradura.
>
> (Where is the truth? But the key
> has got lost in an army of doors
> and it's there among the others,
> without
>   ever finding
>   its lock again.)
> (Por fin no hay nadie" ["At Last There Is No One"],
>   p. 334)

The concept of truth appears throughout the book in an indirect form but with greater clarity in "At Last There Is No One," where the poet urgently asks, as before, "Where is the truth?"

Earlier the truth lay in the fusion with the roots of nature, now we find that this integration is possible through solitude. On the shores of Isla Negra, with its marine harmony, Neruda reencounters the possibilities of creative withdrawal:

> Se abre el perfume ciego de la tierra
> y como no hay caminos
> no vendrá nadie, sólo
> la soledad que suena
> con canto de campana.
>
> (The blind perfume of the earth opens
> and since there are no roads
> no one will come, only
> solitude sounding
> like the singing of a bell.)
>   ("At Last There Is No One," p.334)

The bell, a frequent symbol in the *Isla Negra: A Notebook*, indicates the fullness of the sounds, but now it is a music heard in solitude and introspection, it is the encounter of his own internal song, which sounds like the chiming of a quiet bell. The noun "sonata," song for a solo instrument, reiterates this theme. To combine it with the objective "critical," introduces the idea of tension and a questioning of the values proclaimed in the past. As in *Extravagaria*, also revisionist in nature, the language of the poet and the essence of his role are seen as less solemn. In *Sonata crítica* the voice that called to others is compressed and reduced to near silence. The testimonial poet has fallen silent, and his memory has become precarious.

Isla Negra: A Notebook is one of the most important of Neruda's works because it allows us to explore the beliefs and passions of a man who retrospectively examines his career and shows us the quintessential Neruda at age sixty.

Isla Negra is not simply an autobiographical account, but an accumulation of memories that fluctuate between past and present and even forward to an idealized future in a search for a tie with the world. One of the most important aspects of the book is the coherence of its organic movement. It begins with the poet's search for individual roots, he wanders through exotic cities of the Orient and then returns to the breadth of the land, no longer a being apart from it.

The symbol of the rock in *Isla Negra: A Notebook* suggests resistance to change as well as hardening due to the incomprehension of others. Neruda has felt the force of envy and misunderstanding, and must conceal himself behind a rigid mask. No one responds to his questions. It was not from pride that the poet chose solitude, but from defenselessness. Now the poet is a man alone because his enemies have willed it to be so:

> Pregunté a los otros después,
> a las mujeres, a los hombres,
> qué hacían con tanta certeza
> y como aprendieron la vida:
> en realidad no contestaron.
> siguieron bailando y viviendo.
>
> (Afterwards, I asked the others,
> the women, the men,

what they were doing so confidently
and how they learned how to live:
they did not actually answer.
they went on dancing and living.)
　　("Soledad" ["Solitude"], p. 333)

Isla Negra: A Notebook represents the complexity of the poet's mood as he confronts himself through memory and reaffirmation, drawing strength from the roots of an almost mythical past.[5]

Chapter Six
The Odes: Toward a Simpler Form

Most critics of Neruda's work believe that his poetry is characterized by numerous changes of direction from one volume of poetry to the next. This is the case with Neruda's *Odes,* which appear in three consecutive books: *Odas elementales* (1954) (Elementary odes), *Nuevas odas elementales* (1956) (New elementary odes), and *Tercer libro de las odas* (1957) (Third book of odes). Still another volume, *Navegaciones y regresos,* (Navigations and returns) (1959), is also considered to be part of the *Odes* sequence.

In the earlier *Canto general,* the natural setting of the New World and the American man are announced in a grandiloquent rhetoric. That setting is posited as part of a macrocosm in which the poet takes his place as spokesman for a people. In the *Odes,* that same natural setting fits into the microcosmic space of daily reality.

Neruda began to write the *Odes* when the Caracas newspaper, *El Nacional,* edited by his friend, novelist Miguel Otero Silva, asked him to contribute weekly articles. Neruda accepted on the condition that his work not appear in the literary supplement but in the news section. Neruda says: "That is how I published a long history of time, things, artisans, people, fruit, flowers, and life."[1] In the *Odes,* poetry becomes a chronicle of everyday living, since now what is primary is the common man, and, instead of the history of epic proportions told in *Canto general,* Neruda gives us the history of the everyday man.

In the *Canto general* the delight in material and sensual objects is accentuated, and the poet's desire to partake of them is obvious. The poem "Los frutos de la tierra" (Fruits of the earth) in the section "Yo soy" shows the fondness for particular edibles: tomatoes, onions, and bread. The sensual and earthy materialism of the *Odes* is related to Neruda's Marxist ideology. Both books intend to reach people who have little formal education. The concrete language of the *Odes* becomes an essential instrument in his search for a poetry addressed to the simple man.

The "Oda al hombre invisible" ("Ode to the Invisible Man") and the "Oda al hombre sencillo" ("Ode to the Simple Man") both reinforce the new poetic and political ideal of rendering a humanitarian service. In "Oda a la lluvia" ("Ode to the Rain"), Neruda deplores rain for flooding the homes of the poor, and similarly, in "Oda al aire" ("Ode to the Air"), he begs it to run free and not sell itself to pipes that run only to the dwellings of the wealthy. The objects themselves are conceptualized as being the rightful domain of the people. The "Oda al invierno" ("Ode to the Winter") sets up a dichotomy between winter's beauty and the destruction it brings to the poor.

Neruda no longer sings to the imposing mountains or the turbulent Urubamba River but to objects and everyday things: a pair of scissors, the air, an onion, an apple, a dictionary. Everything commonly used in daily life is made highly poetic but without losing its quality as a practical object:

> Quiero que todo
> tenga
> empuñadura
> que todo sea
> taza o herramienta
>
> (I want everything
> to have
> a use
> for everything to be
> coffee cup or tool.)[2]

The poet's wish for everything to have a use, as he says here, indicates a turning point in his concept of poetry. This idea had been expanded before, especially in his essay entitled "Towards an Impure Poetry" where everyday objects are valued. In the *Odes* the utilitarian idea takes on increased force and importance. Just as the poet proclaims that everything is a tool and has a function, he advocates that poetry too become an instrument of pleasure and understanding for all people. There is in the *Odes* a desire to reach plain people through the marvel of daily objects such as oil, butter, salt, and wine and in addition, through objects created by man for his well-being, such as bicycles or woolen socks. A strong evolution is evident from the despairing poetry we saw in the *Residences*. Rather than a new poetic conception, the *Odes* of Neruda introduce a new attitude of perpetual wonderment.

Conscious that his poetry must be consistent with his politics, Neruda speaks in a lingua franca understood by the people. He writes of everyday things in a colloquial and direct manner so that the *Odes* can be read by all, understood by all, and for this reason they have enjoyed an unprecedented popularity. The conflict between artistic poetry and popular poetry arrives at a resolution. Both the common and the specialized reader can find in the *Odes* aesthetic as well as spontaneous enjoyment.

A perfect melding of theme and form characterizes the *Odes*. In ancient Greece and Rome the ode form was intended to praise and magnify that which was already impressive. To Neruda, a humble onion or a bowl of chowder becomes extraordinary and magical, but not because it is a product of nature but because man, through daily use, gives it stature and nobility:

> la tierra
> así te hizo,
> cebolla,
> clara como un planeta,
> y destinada
> a relucir,
> constelación constante,
> redonda rosa de agua,
> sobre
> la mesa
> de las pobres gentes.

> (so did the earth
> create you,
> onion,
> pellucid planet
> destined to glow,
> constant constellation,
> spherical water rose,
> upon
> the table of the poor.)[3]

The "Oda a la cebolla" ("Ode to an Onion") is an excellent example of how a concrete and everyday entity can be enhanced and transformed without losing its original nature. The humble onion becomes an object of light whose physical armature is compared to that of a flower:

> Pétalo a pétalo
> se formó tu hermosura
>
> (Petal by petal
> was your beauty fashioned
> ("Ode to an Onion," p. 126)

Then he proceeds to describe the birth of the onion from the most essential roots in the earth:

> La tierra acumuló su poderío
> mostrando su desnuda transparencia
>
> (Earth assembled with all her might
> Displaying your translucent nudity)
> ("Ode to an Onion," p. 126)

The overlooked onion transcends its own dimensions and becomes almost sublime, not only because it is intrinsically beautiful, but also because it is the essential food of the poor. Neruda's technique consists of announcing the object through a series of ennobling characteristics—the transparency of its skins and the gentle curves of its form—and then adding to these virtues the sustaining and nutritive power of the object in the practical realm.

In the majority of the *Odes* we can see certain patterns that are repeated that give the ode its special structure. The "Oda a los calcetines" ("Ode to Socks") begins by telling a story:

> Me trajo Maru Mori
> un par
> de calcetines
> que tejió con sus manos
> de pastora,
> dos calcetines suaves

            como liebres,
            En ellos
            metí los pies

            (Maru Mori brought me
            a pair
            of socks
            knitted with her shepherdess
            hands,
            two socks soft
            as hares
            I slipped my feet
            into them)
                    ("Ode to Socks," p. 127)

Maru Mori, the wife of the distinguished Chilean painter Camilo Mori, presents the poet with some hand-knitted socks. The personalization of the story and the image of soft-knit socks made by a "shepherdess" set the poem in motion. The parallel images are the woolen threads, made by a shepherdess with "twilight threads," and sheep skin.

The stockings warm the feet of the poet, which are compared to "two woolen fish," an image that conveys the idea of movement. After this description, it is explained that despite the celestial beauty of these socks, he uses them and gives them life. His feet become the lining of the splendid socks, which are objects of aesthetic delight, human pleasure, and utility.

Inanimate domestic objects, transformed by the poetic eye, take on a new meaning. Neruda pays tribute to them and to the women whose domestic labors had gone too long unnoticed. We see this especially in the "Oda a una lavandera nocturna" ("Ode to a Nocturnal Washerwoman") where the lowly task of scrubbing worn underwear belonging to others is understood as being no less important than other labors of mankind.

In his praise of simple things Neruda makes the form harmonize with the theme. The poems are written in blank verse and in conversational language, but still preserve the tradition of the ode as a civic expression. The lines are brief, sometimes one word long, and the layout of the poem also matches the theme.

The written image and the spoken word work together to create a most satisfying auditory and visual rhythm. The ode is a spiral that unravels as we read. Fernando Alegría explains why Neruda finds in the ode the adequate form for his new concept of poetry. He says, "Neruda uses a peculiarly short, irregular line, not out of mere whimsy but because he believes this type of line performs a definite functional purpose."[4]

René de Costa states that the ode follows a process of enunciation, transformation, and reasoning.[5] First the theme, then its metaphor, and finally the ordinary object—socks, a chestnut, or an apple— is transformed into something extraordinary. We might add that there is also a process of immediate identification with the object so that it becomes quickly domesticated. Thus the object is given new life, and inanimate objects like socks, when touched by man, become humanized.

Neruda's basic concept in the *Odes* is that poetry must be shared by the human family, without exclusions or discriminations. As he said in his Nobel acceptance speech: "A menudo expresé que el mejor poeta es el hombre que nos entrega el pan de cada día: el panedero más próximo que no se cree dios" ("I have often mentioned that the best poet is he who prepares our daily bread: the nearest baker, who does not imagine himself to be a god"). In the same speech, Neruda states that: "Cada uno de mis versos quiso instalarse como un objeto palpable. Cada uno de mis poemas pretendió ser un instrumento útil de trabajo." ("Each and every one of my verses has chosen to take its place as a tangible object. Each and every one of my poems has claimed to be a useful working instrument").[6]

The *Odes* were well received by critics as well as by the common readers that Neruda wished to reach. He had succeeded in exchanging the idea of hermetic poetry addressed to an elite for a poetry of daily use in which form and content come together. Later on, his compatriot Nicanor Parra, would also take up the cause of combating rhetorical language and would champion the use of everyday conversational language in poetry.

In the *Odes* Neruda sang to vegetables in recipes, as well as to people who work in mines or pharmacies. The poet wishes to know all in order to share and disseminate:

> Tengo una obligación terrible
> y es saberlo,
> saberlo todo,
> día y noche saber

> cómo te llamas,
> ese es mi oficio.
>
> (I have a terrible obligation
> to know everything,
> to know night and day
> what your name is,
> that is my calling.)[7]

In referring to his poetry as his "calling," Neruda is indicating that he is no longer enthralled with hermetic poetry as in the *Residences* or the egocentric soliloquies of the love poems. He dedicates himself to reaching the anonymous voiceless people who fill the streets of every city without being noticed. The poet demands to know the details of their lives since there must be no distance between the subject that inspires creation and the creator himself:

> Como tu andas
> como, tu comes
> tengo en mis brazos a mi amor
> como a tu novia, tú.
>
> (How you walk
> how you eat
> I have my love in my arms
> like you have yours.)
>
>   ("Oda al hombre sencillo," ["Ode to the Simple
>   Man"], Nascimento ed., p. 169)

Neruda shows a special predilection for tiny things such as bees or essential substances such as salt. With respect to the poet-philosopher's role, Neruda does not pontificate or profess to know great truths. He simply wants to comprehend, as in "Ode to the Invisible Man." Complementary to this ode, the "Ode to the Simple Man" defends the poet from those who look down upon him for turning towards prosaic and direct expression. Some critics have mistakenly identified Neruda as the philosopher-poet reigning over the subjects on planet earth. But more than a poet-philosopher, Neruda is a poet-citizen, first among equals, whose mission is to praise all creation and present each object as if it were being seen for the first

time. The first principle of the poet's mission is accessibility to all
readers:

> Yo quiero
> que todos vivan
> en mi vida
> y canten en mi canto
>
> (I want
> that all of you live in my life
> and sing in my song)
> ("Ode to the Invisible Man," Nascimento ed.,
> p. 202)

The second principle is the poet as a popular minstrel, like his
contemporary, the Chilean folksinger Violeta Parra, who always
thought of singing as communal sharing. The word *canto* (song) is
consistent with the idea of reaching everyone. Violeta Parra, in one
of her most famous songs, "Gracias a la vida" (Thanks To life), says,
"the song you sing is mine too."[8] The comparison of Neruda with
Parra is relevant and necessary here because the *Odes* have the same
broad impact on the reading public that she had on the listening
public.

Just as *Twenty Love Poems* and the *Residences* had from their in-
ception an immediate impact in the other Spanish-speaking countries, the *Odes,* too, were an instant success. Experienced readers as
well as novices accepted the new structure, style, and images. The
Odes also open the way for the protest song of the 1960s and for
dramatic adaptations of poems by Nicanor Parra, Ernesto Cardenal,
Roque Dalton, and Violeta Parra. Neruda, in advocating a simpler,
down-to-earth poetry, leads the way to new avenues in Spanish-
American poetry.

In the *Odes* Neruda proclaims himself to be a realistic poet, one
no longer immersed in verbal opulence for its own sake. Transitory
and breakable objects regain their beauty, as in the book *Navegaciones
y regresos* (Navigations and returns), where Neruda enumerates the
things that he loves—cups, rings, soup bowls, hats, thimbles,
spurs, plates, vases, and eyeglasses: all objects fashioned by men.
To read an ode is to enter a space where domestic objects speak and
the poem exults in hope and possibilities of life.

The *Odes* represent a process of reconstruction in which an object is examined almost microscopically, transformed into a luminous entity, and elevated to the extraordinary. Like Aphrodite born of the sea, the onion is born of the earth. There is nothing artificial or farfetched in the parallel. Both show nature in its most quintessential forms. The *Odes* reveal the universe to the reader and when recited, to the listeners, as if we were seeing it for the first time in its true meaning. A watch recalls the heartbeat of the beloved, a day on the beach, and at the same time the poetry of fishermen returning from the sea, the miners, the poor washerwomen. The *Odes* as a totality are a celebration in song:

> el canto del hombre invisible
> que canta con todos los hombres
>
> (the song of an invisible man
> singing with all men.)
> ("Ode to the Invisible Man," Nascimento ed.,
> p. 204)

Nonetheless, the reception of the *Odes,* initially so enthusiastic, begins to cool in response to the undeniable repetitions in the four volumes. It is the style that becomes monotonous and not the subjects, which are quite varied.

In the *Odes,* Neruda conceives of poetry as an offering for the utilitarian good of a society. In the evolution of Neruda's poetry the *Odes* represent a new beginning. They break away from hermetic lyrics comprehensible only to a few and focus on the inanimate world of common objects, so common they are most often taken for granted. But the *Odes* are spent by their repetitious simplicity. With the publication of the collection *Estravagaria (Extravagaria)* Neruda recaptures his audience.

Extravagaria

It is not until the last poem of the collection called *Extravagaria*[9] that Neruda states his poetic credo:

> Mientras se resuelvan las cosas
> aqui dejé mi testimonio,
> mi navegante estravagario

> para que leyéndolo mucho
> nadie pudiera aprender nada,
> sino el movimiento perpetuo
> de un hombre claro y confundido,
> de un hombre lluvioso y alegre,
> enérgico y otoñabundo.
>
> (While things are settling down,
> here I've left my testament,
> shifting extravagaria,
> whoever goes on reading it
> will never take in anything
> except the constant moving
> of a clear and bewildered man,
> a man rainy and happy,
> lively and autumn-minded.)
>   ("Testamento de otoño" ["Autumn Testament"],
>   p. 302)

In these verses, Neruda sums up his new poetic attitude. The "extravagario" ("vagar-wander") is an instrument that helps the poet navigate through life and through poetry. But his voyage begins with no definite destination and ends with no absolute certainties. This idea of coming up with no answers to the ultimate questions differs markedly from his earlier stance expressed in the *Canto general,* the poet as social activist and prophet of oppressed peoples. Also, it differs from the civic poet of hope who came forward in the *Odes.* Once again, Neruda is a man like all others, who contradicts himself and suffers doubts. This is the dialectical spirit of the book.

All the categories of the past vanish, but Neruda continues to celebrate simple things, though without hyperbole. In "Pastoral," ("Pastoral") for example, Neruda returns to the wonderment of nature and its transparency, but without the absolute certainty of his role as a seer. Neruda himself is the ordinary man who begins to examine himself:

> Yo también quiero verme,
> quiero saber al fin cómo me siento
>
> (I too want to watch myself,
> I want to discover at last my own feelings)
>   ("Pastoral," p. 119)

We see a poet whose only desire is to answer his own voice. In
"El miedo" ("Fear"), he says:

> Tengo miedo de todo el mundo,
> del agua fría, de la muerte.
> Soy como todos los mortales,
> inaplazable.
>
> (I am afraid of the whole world,
> afraid of cold water, afraid of death.
> I am as all mortals are,
> unable to be patient.)
>
> ("Fear," p. 56)

The poet's withdrawal into the peace and silence of solitude is
one of the governing ideas of this book and of the major portion of
Neruda's posthumous poetry:

> Por una vez sobre la tierra
> no hablaremos en ningún idioma,
> por un segundo detengámosnos,
> no movamos tanto los brazos.
> II
> Sería un minuto fragrante,
> sin prisa, sin locomotoras,
> todos estaríamos juntos
> en una quietud instantánea.
>
> (For once on the face of the earth,
> let's not speak in any language;
> let's stop for one second,
> and not move our arms so much.
> II
> It will be an exotic moment
> without rush, without engines,
> we would all be together
> in a sudden strangeness.)
>
> ("A callarse," "Keeping Quiet," p. 27)

The same solitude that proved so anguishing for him in the
Residences is transformed into something that he desires, not so much
as a rejection of others but as a desire to rediscover and explore
himself:

Ahora me dejen tranquilo,
ahora se acostumbran sin mí.
Yo voy a cerrar los ojos.

(Now they can leave me in peace,
and grow used to my absence.
I am going to close my eyes.)
("Pido silencio," "I Ask for Silence," p. 18)

What is interesting in this poem more than the request for silence, which would imply a search for serenity, is the longing for the elements of the earth that appear in his earlier poetry, such as rain, water, the eyes of the beloved, except now Neruda wishes to share them in silence with his loved one, Matilde.

The poet is asking for silence but not for death:

pero porque pido silencio
no crean que voy a morirme:
me pasa todo lo contrario:
sucede que voy a vivirme.

(because I ask for silence,
don't think I am going to die.
The opposite is true;
it happens I'm going to live.)
("I Ask for Silence," p. 19)

The poet shuns the grandiloquence associated with his poetry and his public image. In addition, he is discovering once more the insufficiency of words for the kind of communication he seeks. This is clearly seen in the poem "Demasiados nombres" ("Too Many Names") in which the earth has no names and thus is immune to classification and delimitation. After working towards simplification of the word and clarity of message in the *Odes,* Neruda now admits that he has no further answers. He even mocks his previously vaunted omniscience:

No le pregunto a nadie nada.
Pero sé cada día menos.

(Now I question nobody.
But I know less every day.)
("And How Long Does it Live"["Y cuánto vive"],
p. 22)

In another poem, "No tan alto" ("Not So Tall") (p. 52), "Si quieren, no me crean nada" ("If you like, don't believe me at all"), he shows that poetry need not be solemn. It can imply an interplay of words in which the poet can change the order of things without claiming to possess any truth. It also implies a revisionist attitude with respect to the poetic and personal past:

> Ahora me doy cuenta que he sido
> No sólo un hombre sino varios
>
> (Now it dawns on me that I have been
> not just one man but several
> ("Regreso a una ciudad" ["Return to a City"], p. 32)

Extravagaria is a recapitulation of many of Neruda's experiences and earlier themes, but the tone that was once so solemn has changed. In the *Odes,* form and content were elaborately fitted together. In *Extravagaria,* the language is absolutely colloquial and direct, like Nicanor Parra's book *Poemas y antipoemas (Poems and Antipoems),* published in 1954. First Parra and then Neruda attack the sacralization of the poet. Parra's words indicate a repudiation of complicated and abstract poetry "in dark glasses." The antipoet proposes clarity above all. Neruda without doubt is influenced by Parra's language and use of irony as a tool:[10]

> Yo soy profesor de la vida,
> vago estudiante de la muerte
> y si lo que sé no les sirve
> no he dicho nada, sino todo.
>
> (I'm a professor of life,
> a vague student of death
> and if what I know is no use
> I have said nothing and everything.)
> ("Not So Tall," p. 52)

His self-parody, like his answer to critics of his changing poetry in "Answers to Well-Meaning People," indicates that *Extravagaria* is full of humor and nothing is taken too seriously, not even the poet himself. The absurd, the comic, and the banal are the only possible approaches to self-awareness. In "Parthenogenesis" the poet isn't sure if he should be forgetful or respectful, and the title has nothing to do with the content of the poem. In "Not So Tall" he contradicts himself, saying "Sin duda todo está muy bien / y todo está muy mal, sin duda" ("No doubt, everything is fine / and everything is very bad, no doubt") (p. 52) and continues playing with language in an almost childlike manner. This is perhaps the greatest change in Neruda's poetry where the verbal reverberation turns into concreteness and nakedness of expression. As David P. Gallagher points out, Neruda's *Extravagaria* phase is an entirely hedonistic one where the poems can not only be about fun, but can be fun.[11]

Neruda's styles and themes are diverse, and the only constant is the similarity of language to the sounds and rhythms of street conversations. In this sense, the accessibility to colloquial language, formulated in the *Odes,* continues here. Alliteration is effectively used in a long poem dedicated to Santiago, "Cantasantiago," where the city's name is altered to "sintigo" ("without you"), an impossible contraction parallel to the legitimate "contigo" ("with you").

When *Extravagaria* appeared in 1958 the idea of playfulness was emphasized by many drawings and illustrations, such as one by Jules Verne and another, of a dancing skeleton, by the celebrated Mexican graphic artist Posada. On one page we read: "Para subir al cielo se necesitan" ("To rise to the sky you need"). Only by turning the page does the reader find out what he needs:

> dos alas,
> un violín,
> y cuantas cosas
> sin numerar, sin que se hayan nombrado
>
> (two wings,
> a violin,
> and so many things, things without names)
> ("To Rise to the Sky," p. 15)

Neruda follows in the tradition of Apollinaire's graphic poems, the surrealists, concrete poetry, and Nicanor Parra's eleven-syllable colloquial poems. *Extravagaria* synthesizes a long line of poets who join language to the visual. The creative use of the space on a page allows reader and poet to unite symbiotically, accepting illogic and incongruence.

In an interesting and revealing poem, Neruda reveals that he has stopped classifying things:

> Yo pienso confundir las cosas,
> unirlas y recién nacerlas,
> entreverarlas, desvestirlas,
> hasta que la luz del mundo
> tenga la unidad del océano,
> una integridad generosa,
> una fragancia crepitante.
>
> (I have a mind to confuse things,
> unite them, and make them new-born,
> mix them up, undress them,
> until all light in the world
> has the oneness of the ocean,
> a generous, vast wholeness,
> a crackling, living fragrance.)
> ("Too Many Names," p. 236)

Confusing things is another way of enunciating a poetic manifesto according to which the division into acceptable and unacceptable is challenged. To accomplish this, Neruda constantly shuffles disparate ideas and images. "Bestiario" best reflects the tone Neruda adopts, saying that one can live quite well "with flies," echoing Parra's *Antipoem* that says "perhaps flies are angels."

Neruda was very fond of his *Extravagaria* and in his *Memoirs* declares it one of his best-loved books. In "Testamento de otoño" ("Autumn Testament") we find the idea that the poet is free once more to be transparent. He brings up the subject of death and counts his earthly possessions, his enemies, and his friends. The "Autumn Testament" paints the poet's self-portrait as "la historia de un hombre claro, confundido, lluvioso, alegre, enérgico, otoñabundo" ("the story of a man, transparent, confused, rainy, happy, energetic and autumn-like")—just as the last section of the *Canto* "Yo soy" (I am) is a kind of last will and testament.

Neruda plays, questions, contradicts, and shows his vulnerability, asking humorously "¿Cúal es cúal, cúal es el cómo? ¿Qúien sabe cómo conducirse?" ("What is the which, which is the how? Who knows how to behave?") ("Sobre mi mala educación," "On My Bad Education," p. 120). It is a benevolent, unsarcastic humor based on incongruencies and word play. *Extravagaria* is a brilliant collection of personal poems where the poet need only answer to himself, ignoring the critics who make him an increasingly controversial figure. It is a book of contemplation of simple things around him and of self-contemplation as well, of the fifty-two-year-old Neruda reflecting on his life. In this revisionistic attitude towards his poetry and his craft lies the key to *Extravagaria*.

We might speculate that each of Neruda's poetic cycles responds to changes in his concept of himself and his surroundings. In the *Canto general* poetry was the chronicle of natural and human history, that of the marginal domains of Latin America, where collective experience merges with personal perception and rediscovery of the beauties of elemental reality. In *Extravagaria* as in the *Odes,* Neruda cultivates a prosaic discourse that can question, doubt, and poke fun in a melancholy way at himself, but without judgmental severity. Though besieged by the enigmas of existence and its imperfections, Neruda reconciles himself to his eventual condition of poet in the autumn of life. *Extravagaria* represents the extravagant acceptance, amazement, irreverence and incongruity of language with all its possibilities. Neruda, who intends never to copy himself, is constantly revising his stances and making inroads into new expressive possibilities. There is a constant evolution between the *Odes* and *Extravagaria* especially in the colloquial, prosaic tone and attempt to garner appeal.

Extravagaria inaugurates a new period in Neruda's life and work characterized by a return to the self. As he says in the poem "Cierto cansancio" ("A Certain Fatigue"), which suggests a kind of apathy, he is tired even of remembering and needs a respite from the past. It is this attitude that gives him the readiness to begin his last phase.

Chapter Seven

Silence and Solitude:
The Posthumous Poetry

Any posthumous poetry poses the question of whether the author has had the time to revise and put his writings in order. This is the case of the eight posthumous books of Pablo Neruda that were published almost simultaneously in 1973, and whose order is the following: *La rosa separada* (The separate rose), *Jardín de invierno* (Winter garden), *2000, El corazón amarillo* (The yellow heart), *El libro de las preguntas* (The book of questions), *Elegía* (Elegy,) *El mar y las campanas* (The sea and the bells) and *Defectos escogidos* (Selected failings). However, this order, which the poet himself preferred, was altered after Neruda's death and therefore they appeared in different years. *El mar y las campanas* was the first to be published.

In this chapter, we will not follow the order of publication or the order chosen by the poet but treat the posthumous books according to thematic coherence, concentrating principally on *La rosa separada* (1973), *El mar y las campanas* (1973), and *Jardín de invierno* (1974).

The language used in the posthumous poetry becomes progressively more simple, taking on an even more prosaic quality than the *Odes* or *Extravagaria.* The rich metaphors of the early poetry and the transparency of the highly lyrical language are left behind. Throughout these poems we find no easily identifiable poetic unity, as there used to be in the *Residences,* the *Odes,* or the *Canto general.* These verses can almost be read separately, as if each book were made up of separate poems with no unifying theme. It is important to mention this, since Neruda is a poet of books and not poems. The reverse occurs in his posthumous poetry. It would seem that these books form part of an unconcluded collection, from which the ill-crafted poems have not been eliminated. Still, they too are important since they are the last work of the poet.

The dominant aspect of the posthumous poetry is introspection.[1] Now near death, Neruda commences a process of hermetic self-contemplation in which his self is the essential poetic material to be rediscovered. This man who was for so many years the lyric spokesman of others, now fatigued, decides to seclude himself within the confines of his rapidly fading persona. He excuses himself for his omissions and bids farewell to all those who, for so many reasons, could not be part of his final verses. His poetic apologia reveals his continuing concern for his fellow men:

> Pero no tuve tiempo ni tinta para todos,
> O bien el menoscabo de la ciudad, del tiempo,
> el frío corazón de los relojes
> que latieron cortando mi medida,
> algo pasó, no descifré,
> no alcancé todos los significados:
> pido perdón al que no esté presente.

> (But I didn't have time or ink for all,
> or maybe the disdain of city and time,
> the chilly heart of clocks
> that pulsated and cut short my measure,
> something happened, I couldn't decipher,
> I missed some of the meanings:
> I apologize to anyone I may have left out.)[2]

The poems of greatest relevance in Neruda's posthumous poetry are those in which, like the one just quoted from *Jardín de invierno,* the realm of personal experience predominates over political ideology, the social poems of *2000,* and the varied poems of *El corazón amarillo.*

La rosa separada, El mar y las campanas, and *Jardín de invierno* form a trilogy with a common perspective: the aging poet nearing the other shore is delineated as a solitary figure seeking communion with nature, especially with the sea and the sand. The anticipation that the present will vanish because approaching death will return him to nature allows him to contemplate his mortality with serenity and acceptance.

These three books permit us to sketch the figure of Neruda, walking toward that same sea that beckoned to him so powerfully in all his poetry, and that will take him out of his suffering. Nonetheless, these books are not the tragic, morose work of a man near death but a man at peace with himself, his life, and his imminent end.

La rosa separada

After his return from Paris in 1971, Pablo Neruda travels to Easter Island (Rapa Nui in the indigenous language), a remote site in the Pacific that belongs to Chile, where the gigantic and strange anthropomorphic sculptures planted on the green expanses of the island stand as a backdrop to the sea. In this book, however, Neruda sees no fusion of man with nature but a fragmentation reflected in the book's division into "Los hombres" (The men) and "La isla" (The island). *La rosa separada* is a book of disjunctions between men and nature. "La isla" is purity, intuition, and uncorrupted earth. "Los hombres" are the awkward, heavy, inopportune creatures who crowd onto the island:

> Somos torpes los transeúntes, nos atropellamos
> de codos,
> de pies, de pantalones, de maletas,
> bajamos del tren, del jet de la nave, bajamos
> con arrugados trajes y sombreros funestos.
> Somos culpables, somos pecadores.
>
> (We are awkward and heavy, we crowd with elbows,
> feet, trousers, and valises,
> we descend from train, jet, ferry, we step down
> with wrinkled suits and deadly hats
> we are guilty, we are sinners.)[3]

Throughout *La rosa separada,* men are defined as "pobres hombres," victims of their silent daily tedium and their colorless lives, who hope for promotions, publications, discussions, and acceptance by an elite of monotonous established values. The island is just the opposite of these humans. It is a separate rose in a garden, in a wild mythical surrounding made for and by the gods. The men prefer to remain separate from the island, which is metaphorically identified with primeval matter and the uncontaminated purity of nature. For this reason, the poet, like the rest, abandons this place:

> Y ésa es mi cobardía, aquí doy testimonio:
> no me sentí capaz sino de transitorios
> edificios, y en ésta capital sin paredes
> hecha de luz, de sal, de piedra y pensamiento,
> como todos miré y abandoné asustado
> la limpia claridad de la mitología.
> las estatuas rodeadas por el silencio azul.
>
> (And that is my cowardice,
> I take my oath here:
> I was only capable of transitory
> buildings, and in this capital without walls
> made of light, salt,
> stones and thoughts,
> like the rest, I gazed and left,
> frightened by the luminous mythology
> the statues surrounded by blue silence.)
>   (Los hombres XIX" [The men XIX], p. 90)

The poet, united with the alienated men he used to criticize, is seen here as indecisive, vacillating, and tangled within himself, alien to that universe of silent stones and mysteries, so he returns to the city, having learned nothing, enveloped in desolate sadness:

> Sino un vacío oceánico, una pobre pregunta
> con mil contestaciones de labios desdeñosos
>
> (And oceanic void, a pitiful question
> with a thousand answers out of disdainful lips)
>   ("Los hombres XIV," p. 70)

Rapa Nui and Macchu Picchu, two monuments in Latin American history, are seen by one poet, but through different prisms. Macchu Picchu in the 1950s represents the integration of a wild and beautiful nature and a personal credo sung by the poet. Rapa Nui is seen in its beauty and mystery, secluded but separate from men who in no way represent Latin America but rather a universal condition born of bourgeois shackles, tedium, and tourism. The poet, too, is part of that human mass that has arrived on the island only to invade and to increase the human pollution. In poem 3, the poet says to the ancient Rapa Nui:

Antigua Rapa Nui, patria sin voz,
perdónanos a nosotros los parlanchines del mundo:
hemos venido de todas partes a escupir en tu lava

(Ancient Rapa Nui, country without voice,
forgive us bubblers of the world:
we have come from everywhere to spit on your lava)
("La isla III" [The island III], p. 21)

Spittle, synonymous with violation and devastation by the men who bring to the island their conflicts and differences, is the very antithesis of the pure volcanic lava of Easter Island.

The poet's response to this conflict between men and the natural world is to take refuge in solitude and in contemplation of his experience, far from that modern world of bitter discussions, wars, and disease.

Jardín de invierno

Silence and seclusion are the leitmotivs of *Jardín de invierno.* If he was "otoñabundo" ("autumnful") in *Extravagaria,* now he is in the winter of his life. He alludes to that last season just as the nocturnal images of *One Hundred Love Sonnets* anticipated it twenty years before. In the title poem we find the expression of awareness of the life cycle:

Soy un libro de nieve,
una espaciosa mano, una pradera,
un círculo que espera,
pertenezco a la tierra y a su invierno.

(I am a book of snow,
a spacious hand, a meadow,
a circle that waits,
I belong to the earth and its winter.
("Jardín de invierno," p. 51)

In this stanza we find the characteristics we mentioned earlier as inherent in the posthumous poetry: the serene resignation of a man who knows that his days are numbered and that he will return to the eternal regenerating earth. Neruda associates death with the primitive doctrines that propound a return to those roots. Therefore, death is not an end but a continual rebirth. In another poem, "Con Quevedo en primavera" (With Quevedo in spring), we find the concept of a nature that germinates and surrounds all living things in juxtaposition to the poet who vainly seeks spiritual regeneration. This concept is described in terms of the night, the snow, and other metaphors associated with winter's passing. That longing indicates a continuous proliferation of infinite springs to come:

> Primavera exterior, no me atormentes,
> dame por hoy el sueño de las hojas
> nocturnas, la noche en que se encuentran
> los muertos, los metales, las raíces,
> y tantas primaveras extinguidas
> que despiertan en cada primavera.

> (External spring, don't torment me,
> give me today the slumber of the nocturnal
> leaves, the night of the dead, the metals,
> and the roots, And so many extinguished Springs
> that awaken each spring.)
> ("Con Quevedo en primavera," p. 32)

The "extinguished spring" germinating once more in the precincts of death recalls previous poems in which spring gives life and love. Here we have one of the central aspects of *Jardín de invierno*. In this context death is only a passing state. In the posthumous poetry, Neruda does not depart from the poetic theme present in all his books: nature as a redemptive force and the integration of man with the universal cycle that intertwines life with death.

Another recurrent motif in this book is the desire for solitude not as an escape from other men but as a state of preparation for the union with nature. In this properly titled collection, the poet seeks to comprehend forces, like the sea and the earth, that will become part of himself. The first poem of *Jardín de invierno* exemplifies this state of mind. There he says:

> No falta nadie en el jardín. No hay nadie:
> sólo el invierno verde y negro, el día
> desvelado como una aparición

(No one is missing in the garden. No one is there:
only the green and black winter, the day
wide awake like an apparition,)
                    ("El egoista" [The selfish one], p. 9)

At the end of the poem he asks that no one intrude on his need
for solitude, his only remaining refuge from "institutions, medals,
and propositions."

Still, with that same desire for solitude and peace comes guilt,
for in *Canto general* Neruda proclaimed himself the poet of communion with man. At the end of the poem his ambivalence becomes
more evident and for a moment we glimpse the pained Neruda of
the *Residence* cycle:

> Y hay un olor de soledad aguda,
> de humedad, de agua, de nacer de nuevo:
> qué puedo hacer si respiro sin nadie
> ¿porqué voy a sentirme malherido?

> (And there is a scent of sharp solitude
> humidity, and birth water again
> what can I do if I breathe with no one,
> why should I feel wounded?)
>   ("El egoista," p. 9)

In comparing solitude to water, humidity, and amniotic fluid,
and linking man to the cycles of nature, Neruda comes full circle
thematically. But the tour de force in this poem is that the same
elements do not act as integrating forces but entropic ones. The
poet's pain comes precisely from those elements in his poetry that
earlier were its essential strength.

In a poem dedicated to the sea, "Llama el océano" (The call of
the sea) the poet, from afar, imagines and brings forth the sea of
his country, since the poem is written while Neruda is ambassador
to France. The expatriate Neruda refuses the alien sea of foreign
cities and longs to die in his country, facing the beach at Isla Negra.
It is a prophetic poem because his wish was fulfilled.

> No, yo me niego al mar desconocido,
> muerto, rodeado de ciudades tristes,

> (No, I refuse the unknown, dead,
> sea, surrounded by sad cities,)
> ("Llama el océano," p. 44)

This poem also presents a duality of the sea that awaits the poet near his native land and death that wants to pull him away. The sea, for Neruda, is a site of cosmic reconciliation and transubstantiation. Another important poem that alludes to the return to the sea and the homeland is "Regreso," (Return). The last stanza is particularly revealing:

> la tierra envuelta en sombras y destellos
> y la copa del mar bajo mis labios.

> (the earth wrapped in shadows and glimmers
> and the wineglass of the sea touching my lips.)
> ("Regreso," p. 60)

This poem has been analyzed both by Jaime Alazraki and Manuel Durán.[4] For both critics the idea of the wineglass sea is related to the Nerudian concept of diving into his own being as if he were diving into the sea. Alazraki believes that the marine images of the poem refer to the concept of total unity of nature and man: from that unity peace filters through. For Neruda it is a peace that leaves him facing a deep well. The well might be death but that no longer matters. Life and the world have now been incorporated with the being that breaks itself like a crystal shell on the rock, and in the blow, as in a flash of lightning, life glimmers in its incommensurable unity.

When the glass is destroyed and spilled Neruda begins the entry into another stage of equal cosmic force—the death that, despite its potential for annihilation, can be regeneration.

Jardín de invierno keeps its essential unity throughout, centered on the personal reality of the poet and his destiny, with the exception of the poem, "Otoño," (Autumn) in which he speaks of the last days of the Allende government. Here it seems that the political Neruda, the friend and defender of the people, returns from self-contemplation for a brief moment to denounce a new injustice.

The introspective poems, with their desire to be alone in the

garden, are a way for the poet to prepare himself for merging himself
with other men, with matter, and with the vast sovereignty of the
sea: "Ya no hay más estrella que el mar" (Now there is no star
except the sea) ("La estrella," Star, p. 95).

El mar y las campanas

Solitude, silence, and introspection are the recurrent motifs of
this collection that, with *La rosa separada* and *Jardín de invierno,*
comprises a thematic trilogy in Neruda's posthumous poetry. In
addition there are also numerous associations with sound and music
in *El mar y las campanas:*[5]

> Gracias violines, por este día
> de cuatro cuerdas. Puro
> es el sonido del cielo
> la voz azul del aire.
>
> (Thanks violins for this day
> of four chords. Pure
> is the sound of the sky
> the blue voice of air.)
>   ("Gracias, violines" [Thanks violins], p. 13)

Neruda attributes to the sky its own sound and to the air, its
particular voice. Nature and the day fuse in the musical metaphor
of these lines. This cryptic poem presents the essential ideas found
in *El mar y las campanas.*

The counterpoint to the theme of music is the theme of silence,
that silence necessary for the comprehension of the flow of time. In
the poem that begins the collection, we read:

> El hombre espera
> y sólo
> su campana
> allí está entre las otras
> guardando en su vacío
> un silencio implacable
>
> (Man waits
> and only
> his bell

> rings above the others
> keeping in its emptiness
> an implacable silence)
> ("Inicial" [Initial], p. 7)

Man can find his voice in meditative introspection.

In "Salud decimos cada día" (We say 'cheers' every day), there is another type of silence, the false one of empty and meaningless words:

> Se oye bien, existimos.
> Salud, salud, salud,
> éste y al otro, a quien,
> y al cuchillo al veneno.
>
> (You hear it clearly, we exist,
> Cheers, cheers, cheers,
> to this one and that one
> and the other one
> and to the poisoned knife.)
> ("Salud decimos cada día," p. 25)

It is this atmosphere that the poet wishes to escape, that sonorous emptiness "como para cegar o ensordecer" (that can blind or deafen) ("Les contaré" [I will tell you], p. 36). Thus, in alluding to the false silence, Neruda says "Hace tiempo que no escucho nada" (I haven't heard anything for a while) ("Les contaré," p. 36). In "Quiero saber" (I want to know) again we have the desire for a perfect silence far from the wordly noise of men and to a certain extent, the desire not to speak. The poet opts for nonverbal communication or for saying nothing since speech only serves to "introduce merchandise," like the colonizers who "cambiando baratijas por silencio" (exchanged trinkets for silence) ("Quiero saber," p. 59).

In *El mar y las campanas* there is sharp criticism of language that says nothing, that is filled with cavities and voids. Neruda proposes that one will realize himself in quietude and interior truth.

Pablo Neruda, at the end of his days, executes a profound critique of the craft of the word that only obscures communication, or words like nets that only entangle the content and lead to a vacuum, to nowhere:

palabras sin destino
que no van más allá de tú y yo

(words without destination
which go farther than you and I)
("Pedro es el cuando" [Pedro is the when], p. 46)

The dimension of social and political solidarity and the continued commitment to meaning turns this posthumous poetry into a deconstruction of false premises and values. But Neruda always presents an alternative, a new possibility: individual examination of conscience.

The word, used before as a vehicle to denounce suffering and exploitation, becomes a defense of silence. Neruda in using such apparently contradictory images as a bell without sound or a submerged silence, is implying all this. *El mar y las campanas* goes in a direction chosen by many poets such as Mallarmé, whose search led to the concept of a music of silence.

"Se vuelve a yo" (A return to me) synthesizes not only the themes of *El mar y las campanas,* but all the highly personal and introspective posthumous poetry of Neruda, which uses the personal language of *Extravagaria* but without the playful spirit of that book:

Se vuelve a yo como a una casa vieja
con clavos y ranuras, es así
que uno mismo cansado de uno mismo,
como de un traje lleno de agujeros,
trata de andar desnudo porque llueve,
quiere el hombre mojarse en agua pura,
en viento elemental, y no consigue
sino volver al pozo de sí mismo.

(One returns to the self as if to an old house
with nails and slots, so that
a person tired of himself
like a suit full of holes,
tires to walk nude in the rain,
he tries to take a dip in pure water,
in elemental wind, and cannot
but return to the well of himself.)
("Se vuelve a yo," p. 39)

The tone of reflexive intimacy that predominates in *El mar y las campanas* is particularly evident in this poem. Neruda uses the symbology of the house, with its "tools and slots" to express a dual journey: the physical return to his parental home in Chile and a spiritual return to himself and the origins of his poetic impulses. The image of a suit full of holes, used previously in the famous poem "I Explain a Few Things" of the *Third Residence,* implies a casting off of old ways and creeds that leads the way to a new poetic and political ideology. Also in this poem, the suit full of holes reveals the desire to abandon the old garments of his previous poetry and begin afresh in "agua pura" (pure water). Neruda is in search of transparency and purity: "porque llueve / quiere el hombre mojarse en agua pura" (because it's raining, man wants to drench himself in pure water); yet he knows that the return to virginal immaculateness is a mirage, for one can only return "al pozo de sí mismo" (to the well of one's self).

Once more we see the encounter of man and his solitude, the poet's reencounter with his own essence and a new resurrection that is part of personal regeneration.

El libro de las preguntas

Though the theme of death appears in *El libro de las preguntas,*[6] it is certainly not the prevalent one in this playful book, which, as the title suggests, is written in the form of questions. The style of the collection is brief and cryptic, full of interrogatives written with candor and childlike ingenuousness. The book conveys the vision of the poet in perpetual wonderment at the problems of humanity. There are questions about himself, about the weather, and about philosophy.

Each question corresponds to a certain vision or attitude toward the world such as when he asks himself how many churches there are in heaven. The organization of each poem is difficult to discern, and there are questions on the same page that apparently have nothing to do with each other. All of which gives this text a sense of naïvité, of continual playfulness that makes it delightful to read. In its deceptive simplicity it contains the great metaphors and themes of all times: death, life, rebirth, and all the questions that have no answers. The appeal of the book lies in the marvelous questions that mix the sophisticated poet with the child that he once was:

> Si todos los ríos son dulces
> De dónde saca sal el mar?
>
> (If all rivers are sweet
> Where does the sea get its salt?)
>   (72, p. 94)

Neruda keeps himself open to the memories of his early childhood.
He returns to that incongruent mood of *Extravagaria* or to that
perpetual wonderment initiated in the book of *Odes*. *El libro de las
preguntas* has the exuberance and the wonderment of the *Odes*, where
the abolition of traditional logic is permitted and the poet creates
his own logic:

> No crees que vive la muerte
> Dentro del sol de una cereza?
>
> (Don't you think death lives
> Inside the sunshine of a cherry?)
>   (38, p. 52)

Defectos escogidos, 2000, and *El corazón amarillo* are three of the
books of posthumous poetry that shall be mentioned but not discussed here, since the most important volumes are those already
analyzed. *2000* is a collection of poems attacking the technological
era, and *Elegia* is the recounting of a journey through the Soviet
Union, a country that for years was the ideological center for the
poet. It is interesting to compare some poems of this text with those
dedicated to Russia in the *Third Residence,* like the "Canto a Stalingrado." *El corazón amarillo* is a collection of random poems that
center upon the absurdity of social behavior and convention.

El fin del viaje (Journey's end) and *El río invisible* (The invisible
river) are considered posthumous books in the sense that they appear
after Neruda's death but many of the works in the books were written
at all stages of his life and are simply collected here. Such is the
case of *El río invisible,* a mixture of prose and poetry from the poet's
youth. These books are rendered more comprehensible by the scru-
pulous editing and bibliographical notations of Matilde Urrutia and
Jorge Edwards. *El río invisible* is a true jewel for those interested in
the period of Neruda's adolescence because it contains the seeds of
his conception of the world, tells of his relationships, and his reading.

El fin del viaje is also a collection of dispersed poems culled from a number of Chilean and foreign journals. The book enhances the poet's personality and identifies the people with whom he corresponded. For example, "Elegía para cantar" (Elegy for singing) is a moving poem dedicated to the eminent folklorist Violeta Parra, and the poem "Mujer" (Woman) is dedicated to the washerwoman, women workers, and wives of prisoners, a poem where we see women becoming involved in the social struggle and future political change.

The second part of the text of *El fin del viaje* consists of a section entitled "Paloma por dentro" (Dove inside), which is the original facsimile edition of some poems of *Residence on Earth* with illustrations by Federico García Lorca.

In *El libro de las preguntas* we find the following query:

> No será nuestra vida un túnel
> entre dos vagas claridades?
>
> (Isn't our life a tunnel
> Between two dim clarities?)
> (35, p. 49)

The concept of a tunnel sinking into the self is the essence of this posthumous poetry, written largely in the winter of Neruda's life. But death is not feared but almost welcomed as a time for clarification and, at the same time, the commencement of a new existence where "one returns to the self as to an old house." The house is a space of reflection and introspection, necessary in order to enter into dialogue with the sea and with silence.

The shortcomings of the posthumous poetry are comprehensible if we remember that this is the story of a man tired of being chronicler of others. The posthumous poetry is a clear integration with nature, with that child of the southern forests, with that man who hopes to reintegrate himself with the roots that he believes will nourish him. Therefore the poetry is more personal than ideological.

Neruda's posthumous poetry represents a revisiting of the central motifs of his poetry: the earth, nature, the ocean, immense and vital, a voyage to the interior of the man, where the voice, instead of being explosive and cosmic, becomes introspective and silent:

Porque una vez, porque una voz, porque una
sílaba o el transcurso de un silencio
o el sonido insepulto de la ola
me dejan frente a frente a la verdad,
y no hay nada más que descifrar,
ni nada más que hablar: eso era todo:
se cerraron las puertas de la selva,
circula el sol abriendo los follajes,
sube la luna como fruta blanca
y el hombre se acomoda a su destino.

(Because one time, because one chime, because a
syllable or the passage of a silence,
or the unburied sound of the wave
put me face to face with truth,
and there is nothing more to decipher,
and nothing more to discuss: that was all
the doors of the forest closed,
the sun gravitates and opens the foliage,
the moon rises like white fruit
and man gets used to his destiny.)
("Animal de luz" [Animal of light], p. 78)

Chapter Eight
Neruda and His Critics: An Overview

Criticism on Neruda is as plentiful as his own writing. His poetry allows for such a wide range of interpretations at so many levels that another set of difficulties is created in trying to encompass it. Some critics choose to focus exclusively on the lyrical, personal, and metaphysical aspects of the poetry, especially in the *Residences* and *Isla Negra: A Notebook;* others concentrate exclusively on the political dimensions of Neruda's writing. Still another group of critics judges the sociopolitical content to be of no literary value and therefore ignores it.

In this chapter I will present an overview of the major critical works on Neruda in order to guide the reader in further exploration and research, concentrating on what I consider to be the most useful and coherent analyses of Neruda's poetry.

Criticism on Neruda has tended to follow traditional approaches, including stylistic and thematic analysis based on close readings of individual poems. Despite the large bibliography on Neruda, very little work done to date has been based on the theories of structuralism, poststructuralism, and deconstruction.

Biographical criticism has been popular because of the dramatic nature of Neruda's life. Two biographies may be considered essential. First is *Las vidas de Pablo Neruda* by Neruda's niece and personal secretary for some years, Margarita Aguirre. This book contains the most complete biographical information published to date and constitutes an indispensable portrait of the poet. Aguirre manages to incorporate not only the factual information concerning Neruda's life but also to create a personal, and at times subjective, chronicle of the man and his habits. For example, she tells of his favorite books and his personal pastimes such as contemplating the sea every morning before beginning to write. This biography is not only inspired and original but also carefully structured and documented.

Second to the Aguirre biography is *El viajero inmóvil* by Emir Rodríguez Monegal. This is a documented study of Neruda's poetic trajectory, and it puts forth a number of seminal ideas concerning Neruda's work like the thematic and stylistic unity of the first and second *Residences*. Rodriguez Monegal emphasizes the importance of the poet's early writings, seeing in them the foundation for his subsequent production. In the many textual analyses of key poems in this study, both the personal and the sociopolitical implications are considered, thus allowing Rodríguez Monegal to achieve a fine balance between Neruda's literary and public personae. *El viajero inmóvil* weaves together Neruda's life and artistry and creates a vivid portrait of the poet in this foremost literary biography to date.[1]

The criticism concerning the major works of Pablo Neruda is abundant, and I shall cite those that appear to be most accessible and promising as a basis for future studies. *Pablo Neruda: Naturaleza, historia y poética* by Eduardo Camacho Guizado, written in a simple, accessible style, takes in all of Neruda's major works from the youthful *Crepusculario* to his posthumous poetry. Camacho divides the work into two categories: those works influenced by Spanish-American modernism and the avant-garde and those that reflect social and political ideologies. He analyzes not only the global thematic content of the various collections but also includes specific discussions of important poems. While this study is not excessively erudite, it does present one of the clearest views of the major trends in Neruda's poetic works.

Earth Tones by Manuel Durán and Margery Safir is an excellent source of biographical and literary information on Neruda and is perhaps the most complete book written on the poet in English. The cohesiveness and clarity of the authors' interpretations are due to a great extent to their focus on thematic divisions rather than chronological ones. It is an intimidating task to take on the totality of Neruda's work, but in this book Durán and Safir succeed.

Durán and Safir establish the following classifications of Neruda's work: "The Erotic Poet," "The Nature Poet," "The Public Poetic," "The Personal Poet," and, finally, "The Posthumous Poetry." Each chapter analyzes the particular poetic theme throughout all of Neruda's work while focusing on selected verses that reinforce the general analysis. The reader is given a point of reference as well as a unified trajectory to follow. Durán and Safir differ from other literary critics who have emphasized Neruda's multiple poetic personae. For them Neruda is best seen and portrayed as "a single literary persona expressing his vision through techniques which respond to the diverse changes in his life."[2]

René de Costa in his book, *The Poetry of Pablo Neruda,* stresses not the thematic continuity of Neruda's works but rather his dynamic need for change. In contrast to Durán and Safir, de Costa uses the traditional chronological approach to explore the diverse poetic voices throughout Neruda's production. De Costa's major contribution is to justify the transcendence of the books he studies: *Twenty Love Poems and a Song of Despair,* the *Residences, Canto general,* the *Odes,* and *Extravagaria.*

Another critical approach places Neruda in a universal historical and literary context. The pioneering study in this category is Jaime Alazraki's *Poética y poesía de Pablo Neruda.* Alazraki notes that Neruda's work from 1924 to 1936 is motivated by an aesthetic directly connected with literary developments both in Europe and Spanish America. He discusses the influence of French romanticism on Neruda's early works and also the European avant-garde influence on *Tentativa del hombre infinito* and *Anillos.* One of the most valuable aspects of the book is the explanation of the relationship between Neruda and his literary antecedents, such as Rubén Darío, Carlos Sábat Ercasty, Rabindranath Tagore, and Walt Whitman.

Pablo Neruda: The Poetics of Prophecy by Enrico Mario Santí also places Neruda within a European and Western literary tradition. Santí focuses his attention on the *Residences* and *Canto general,* particularly the poem *The Heights of Macchu Picchu.* Like Alazraki, Santí sees Neruda as a poet abreast of European literary trends. Santí's focus, however, is on what he refers to as the "poetics of prophecy," which is associated with the concept of the poet as seer. He does not consider that the concept of prophecy contradicts Neruda's Marxist ideology. Instead, he demonstrates that the poetry embodies a rhetoric where religion and politics merge "in the unified vision of poet as seer and transformer of reality."[3] The concept of the poet as prophet is synthesized in the chapter dedicated to the *Canto general* where, using examples from the Scriptures, Dante's *Inferno,* and other works, he analyzes Neruda's role as the poet-chronicler in constructing a new Latin American history. Santí's book is recommended, although his zealousness in proving his hypothesis sometimes results in somewhat dogmatic pronouncements.

Another category within Neruda's criticism treats one particular period or collection in detail. This is the case with the masterful book by Amado Alonso, *Poesía y estilo de Pablo Neruda: Interpretación de una poesía hermetica*. Alonso analyzes with unequalled precision the first two *Residences,* paying close attention to language structure, images, symbols, rhythm, and syntax. He also examines the morphological "enjambements," lexicon, and the recurrence of particular symbols. This meticulous analysis serves to reinforce the central thesis of a world in a state of disintegration where the individual survives amid permanent chaos. In a practical application of his method of stylistic criticism, Alonso shows that the incoherent tone and the unique rhythms of the *Residences* reflect the disorientation of Neruda's own life at the time.

El monismo agónico de Pablo Neruda by Alfredo Lozada follows Alonso's critical methodology. In fact, the first part of the book summarizes the principal ideas set forth by Alonso, while the second considers the optimistic tone found at the end of the second *Residences.* Lozada proposes that the thematics of disintegration in the *Residences* culminate with the integration of matter and the cosmos. This recent contribution to criticism on the *Residences* certainly sheds new light on this enigmatic collection.

There are two fundamental books on *Canto general,* one by Juan Villegas, *Estructuras míticas y arquetípicas en el "Canto general,"* and another by Frank Reiss, *The Word and the Stone.* The Villegas book is a mythical and archetypical study, based on the work of Mircea Eliade, Joseph Campbell, and Karl Jung. Villegas bases his analysis on the premise that Neruda's poetic imagination is characterized by a mythifying tendency. One clear example of this is *The Heights of Macchu Picchu,* where Villegas sees the nucleus of the poem as a recounting of the adventures of the mythical hero.

Villegas observes that the mythical consciousness found in the *Canto general* does not contradict the historical materialism implicit in the poem, but that "the very poetic creation of images is mythical sinces the poet confronts the Latin American past and transforms this past, nature, and its world."[4] According to Villegas, some figures of proletarian origin in the poem become mythical heroes while some members of the oligarchy are antiheroes. Neruda himself, as poetic narrator of continental history, takes on the charactistics of a mythical hero who narrates and redeems the history of his continent. According to this critic; "The immediate motivation of

Neruda is the events of his times, the historical conception is that of dialectical materialism; the poetic technique is mythification."[5]

Frank Reiss's book, titled *The Word and the Stone* after a verse from *The Heights of Macchu Picchu*—"una permanencia de piedra y de palabra" ("a permanence of the stone and the word")—exemplifies the analysis used by the author. The "stone" alludes to the nucleus of images that imply infinite time and the "word" refers to the lavish language used in the *Canto*. Reiss uses the structuralist method to analyze the poem as a coherent unity of juxtaposed images. In a detailed manner this British critic studies with precision the reiterated images of the poem. Reiss emphasizes the unitary structure of the *Canto* and brings into his analysis the historical, social, and lyrical dimensions.

Reiss concludes that the most recurrent aspect in *Canto general* is the juxtaposition of opposing images such as land/sea, silence/sound, light/darkness, people/oligarchy. These symmetrical pairs are closely related to the notion of unitary order expressed in the *Canto general*. Among the isolated recurring images, Reiss cites the wave, the rose, the stone, the tree, the root, the snow, and the foam, all of which resonate with multiple associations throughout the *Canto* and appear later on, especially in *One Hundred Love Sonnets*.

Both books form an excellent basis for studying the *Canto general*, with Villegas concentrating on the mythopoetic content and Reiss contributing an original interpretation of the language that gives rise to the mythical and archetypical images.

Other monographic studies of particular works include *Memorial de Isla Negra: Integración de la visión poética* by Luis González Fernández Cruz and a more recent study by the same author on *Tentativa del hombre infinito*. Fernández Cruz examines the *Memorial de Isla Negra* from a thematic point of view, emphasizing the reconstruction of the past through memories.

Jaime Concha and Hernán Loyola have done considerable research on Neruda's social and political poetry. *Ser y morir de Pablo Neruda* by Loyola is one of the fundamental books that treats Neruda's work from the early poems published in local newspapers up through the *Canto general*, that is, from 1918 to 1950. From a Marxist perspective, Loyola weaves biography with literary analysis and relates them to the political and cultural climate of the period. As mentioned earlier, some critics of Neruda have considered the political element as circumstantial, and therefore there are few studies that concentrate specifically on this aspect.

Jaime Concha continues Loyola's Marxist analysis in his book, *Neruda 1904–1936.* He examines the poet's working-class origins and his move to Santiago, where he lived in a bourgeois environment not his own: this fact is reflected in the sense of inadequacy and alienation present in the *Residences.* Concha analyzes in detail the social conditions in Chile in the years 1904–36 and describes the saltpeter crisis in Temuco in 1918 and the mistreatment of the Mapuche Indians of the region. This sociohistorical information reinforces the central thesis that Neruda, from early youth, was drawn towards a Marxian concept of his surroundings. This perspective also explains his lyrical materialism. For example, Concha states that the constant references to wood in Neruda's poetry are not only a poetic allusion but also reflect aspects of his historical reality. Thus, wood is not only a commodity but projects a history of Araucania and its inhabitants, as the freight train driven by Neruda's father through the forested areas of Chile is a concrete example of the combination of nature-history used in his poetry.

Pablo Neruda: All the Poets, the Poet, by Salvadore Bizarro is the only book dedicated exclusively to the social and political poetry of Neruda. Beginning with the poem "Bajo las nuevas banderas" ("Under the New Flags") of the *Third Residence* and proceeding through to *Canto general,* Bizarro studies the intrinsic Marxist ideology found in these works that are addressed to the proletarian reader. Though the book repeats many of the ideas expressed by other critics, it is a concise survey of the political poetry of Neruda.

Neruda's multifaceted poetry and personality are revealed through this critical overview.[6] He is a political and a social poet as well as an intensely lyrical and human one. All the work done to date as well as that which awaits critics in the future is a testimony to the complexity and multiplicity of the poet's genius.[7]

Neruda and His Translators

Neruda is undoubtedly one of the most translated poets of our times. We should note particularly that he is the Latin American poet who has had the greatest impact on English-language poets and translators, especially in the nineteen fifties. Many North Americans, such as Robert Bly and W. S. Merwin, found in the process

of translating Neruda a way to expand their own poetic imagina-
tions.[8] Yet many of these poet-translators do not capture Neruda's
complexity of images and also do not convey the organic energy of
his poetry.

The translation by W. S. Merwin of the *Twenty Love Poems*[9] sac-
rifices many images and does not convey the feeling of desperate
longing found in this early work. Robert Bly's translations of Neruda
in his book *Neruda and Vallejo*[10] emphasize the possibilities of abstraction cultivated in the English language rather than the sensual
images of the Chilean.

Thanks to the work of many translators Neruda became well
known in English-speaking countries especially in the nineteen six-
ties. Before the translations of Bly and Merwin had their impact on
North American poets, the Spaniard Angel Flores published fragments of the *Residences* and *Canto general* under the auspices of the
New Directions publishing house (1946). These were textual translations that did not explore the intricacies of language and meter,
as many other literal translations that followed did.[10] Donald Walsh's
translations of the *Residences* and *The Captain's Verses* also fail to evoke
the lyrical, rhythmic, and imagistic power of Neruda. It is true
that the *Residences* are extremely difficult to translate, but they do,
for this very reason, offer an opportunity for great poetic license and
versatility in the host language. Walsh wrote in his essay "Some
Thoughts on Translation" that:

The translator's role is humble and secondary but nonetheless crucial: to
bring out into his language a work that is worthy of the considerable effort
involved in the act of translation. His goal must be to say in the second
language what the author said in the first language with as much fidelity
as is permitted by the difference in the two languages. And he must do
his best to circumvent the obstacles presented by those differences. His
duty is to express not himself but his author.[11] Although Walsh's translations are faithful to the original Spanish they lack the poetic fantasy and
dreamlike state characteristic of this work.

Ben Belitt, in *Selected Poems* (Grove Press, 1974), the most complete collection of Neruda's poetry in one volume in English, represents the other end of the translating spectrum, in that he takes
so much liberty that he passes over Neruda's meanings, creating
images that did not exist in the original Spanish. Belitt believes

that the translator can be neither anonymous nor literal, like Walsh, and therefore uses Neruda's work as a vehicle for his own expression.

To translate Neruda successfully one must find a balance between literal translation and the imaginative possibilities that the poems offer. *Isla Negra: A Notebook,* translated by Alastair Reid, represents a fine equilibrium of a creative yet faithful translation of Neruda. Reid captures the Proustian sense of memory as well as the striking panorama of the Chilean landscape. Reid himself states that he did most of the translating in Puerto Rico, where the seascape is like the Chilean coastal plane. He understood that a translation of Neruda must go beyond mimesis to search for an equivalent for Neruda's unique tone and sensual effervescence. Neruda himself gallantly commended Alastair Reid for not only translating his poems but bettering them. [12] Reid's translation of *Extravagaria* also captures the playful spirit that characterizes the work.

Other notable translations of Neruda have been done by H. R. Hays (1948) [13] and Nathaniel Tarn (1967), in particular their version of *The Heights of Macchu Picchu,* despite its grammatical and semantical flaws, has the virtue of capturing the poetic ambiguities and imagistic richness of this poem.

Justice is done to Neruda's integral vision in John Felstiner's rendering of *The Heights of Macchu Picchu,* which not only shows a profound intuition of the subtleties and the lyrical vision of the Spanish language, but gives a sense of the historical transcendence. Felstiner tells us that he began the process of translating this poem by journeying to the citadel of Macchu Picchu to imbue himself not only with Neruda's words but with the place that inspired them. Felstiner makes new inroads into the difficult field of literary translation, and his book *Translating Neruda: The Way to Macchu Picchu* in itself is a landmark work. In addition to its theoretical importance, the book contains a well-documented chapter on the history of translations into English of Neruda. Felstiner's work is a model to be followed in future translations of Pablo Neruda into English and other languages.

Given the complexity and the uniqueness of Neruda, it is not surprising that so much of his work remains untranslated in English. Many of his early works, the *Odes,* and all of the posthumous poetry are still untouched. Neruda himself knew that his poetry, so exuberant, so intensely lyrical and at times ambiguous or colloquial, would be hard to translate to other languages, but especially English.

He felt that Italian would be the closest to Spanish because of the melodic similarities.[14] Nevertheless, the translations such as the ones by Nathaniel Tarn, Alastair Reid, and John Felstiner demonstrate that Neruda in English can be as meaningful and powerful as Neruda in Spanish.

Conclusion

The breadth of Neruda's poetry makes it difficult to formulate definitive conclusions. Still, there are certain elements that we shall summarize here.

The natural landscape of Southern Chile, where Neruda spent his childhood, is a presence that we have seen throughout his work. The many paths of his travels converge on the Chilean terrain in a desire to recover his ancestral roots. His search becomes an essential instrument for the development of his imaginative and intuitive grasp of the world. Neruda's poetry in its totality points toward that return to the source, to the woods, the trees, and the Araucanian Indian kingdom.

Together with the return to the primeval forest, the poet longs to imbibe all the natal images such as rain and water, as if to absorb them, for Neruda's poetry is a tapestry that unifies disparate elements, weaving them together in a complete, connected vision. His eroticism, too, is always linked to the concept of the regenerating earth. His poetic symbolism undergoes modifications across time but always retains its telluric childhood imagery.

The vitality and freshness of Neruda's poetry comes from this direct apprehension of the world in its virgin state. Neruda himself recognizes that his poetry is an attempt to flee from abstraction, from all that disconnects us from nature and our fellow men. His poetry began as that of a man estranged and alone, but later it becomes a solid tool that can be shared by all.

Neruda's lyrical evolution is directly connected to his life, as we have said in almost every chapter of this book. Each book we have studied came out of a specific phase of Neruda's life, phases of profound introspection and aloneness interspersed with phases of total involvement with the political and literary life of his time. But in all of his books, Neruda shows a strong awareness of the reader, whose presence hovers like a shadow. The frank dialogue that the reader enjoys with Neruda may account in part for his tremendous popularity. His inmost self is transformed into the collective self, particularly in later works such as the *Canto general*.

To read Neruda is above all a sensual experience, a contact with the humidity of wood and rain, and a vision of the wild landscapes of his beloved country. In reading Neruda we enter the world of a poet who from the beginning has tried to liberate himself from the too rational control of premeditated words and to create a kind of nonliterary literature where intuition and instinct are allowed to survive.

For this reason, from *Crepusculario* to *Residence on Earth,* Neruda's poetry presents visions and metaphors born of an analogical concientiousness in which the reader, too, must participate in an intuitive manner, to see the world and the unexpected in a new way. Neruda is equally capable of being either totally hermetic or totally transparent, but his voice is always authentic. He is always the poet who dares to be, who dares to give himself up to the unknown muse of poetry. For in Neruda all is animation and essence, and his poetry flows in a dynamic that does not bind the reader but bears him away in a state of imaginative rapture.

Notes and References

Chapter One

1. *Memoirs,* trans. Hardie St. Martin (New York, 1977), 6. The *Memoirs* were begun in 1962 and the Brazilian newspaper *O Cruzeiro Internacional* published the section "Las vidas del poeta" in its January-March issue of that year.

2. The information for this chapter comes from the biography of Margarita Aguirre, the poet's niece, *Las vidas de Pablo Neruda* (Santiago: Zig-Zag, 1967). I have also taken some facts from Carlos Hamilton, *Pablo Neruda: Poeta chileno universal* (Santiago, 1972) and Emir Rodríguez Monegal, *El viajero inmovíl* (Buenos Aires, 1966). For a complete and intimate portrait of the poet, see his *Memoirs* and also the interview by Rita Gilbert in *Seven Voices: Seven Latin American Writers Talk to Rita Gilbert* (New York, 1973)), 1-74.

3. The First Journey," in *Isla Negra: A Notebook* (New York, 1970), 6; hereafter cited in text. This and all subsequent quotations from Neruda's works, unless otherwise stated, are translated by Lorraine Roses.

4. Vicente Huidobro, "Ars poética," in *The Selected Poetry of Vicente Huidobro* (New York: New Directions, 1981), 3. For further information on the importance of Vicente Huidobro in the general panorama of Latin American poetry, see Cedomil Goić, *La poesia de Vicente Huidobro* (Santiago de Chile: Universidad de Chile, 1956). David Barry, *Huidobro o la vocación poética* (Granada: Universidad de Granada, 1963). For general works on the avant-garde, see Juan Jacobo Bajarlía, *La poesia de vanguardia: De Huidobro a Vallejo* (Buenos Aires: Losada, 1965), and Renato Poggioli, *The Theory of the Avant-Garde* (Cambridge, Mass: Harvard University Press, 1968).

5. André Bretón. For further information on the surrealists, see Maurice Nadeau, *The History of Surrealism* (New York: Macmillan, 1965); Anna Balakian, *Surrealism: The Road to the Absolute* (New York: Noonday Press, 1959).

6. Neruda publishes this letter on 27 November in the newspaper *El Nacional* of Caracas because in Chile there was press censorship. This letter brought on his political trial.

7. *Toward the Splendid City: Nobel Lecture* (New York: Farrar, Straus & Giroux, 1972), 4.

8. The concept of the poet as artisan is used often by Neruda especially in his *Memoirs* and also in his Nobel Prize speech.

Chapter Two

    1. Hernán Loyola, "Lectura de *Veinte poemas*," in Isaac J. Levy and J. Loveluck, eds., *Simposio Pablo Neruda: Actas* (New York, 1975), 339–53. For further analysis concerning the *Viente poemas* of Pablo Neruda see the following: Eliana Suarez Rivero, *El gran amor de Pablo Neruda* (Madrid, 1971), and Jaime Concha, "Sexo y pobreza," *Revista Iberoamericana* 39, nos. 82–83 (January–June 1973), 135–57. See also the article by Alfredo Losada, "La amada crepuscular," in *Pablo Neruda*, eds. Emir Rodríguez Monegal and Enrico Mario Santí (Madrid, 1980), and Manuel Durán, "Pablo Neruda y la tradición romantica simbolista," *Cuadernos Americanos* 3 (1980): 187–99.

    2. "Body of a Woman," in *Twenty Love Poems and a Song of Despair*, trans. W. S. Merwin (New York, 1983), 8; hereafter cited in text.

    3. *Cartas de amor de Pablo Neruda*, ed. and comp. Sergio Fernández Larraín. (Barcelona: Rodas, 1975).

    4. John Felstiner, "A Feminist Reading of Pablo Neruda," *Parnassus: Poetry in Review* 3, no. 2 (1974): 93. This is the only detailed study to date that concerns the concept of woman in the love poetry of Pablo Neruda.

    5. The information about the history of *The Captain's Verses* is explained in great detail by Margarita Aguirre in *Las Vidas de Pablo Neruda* and in Rodríguez Monegal, *El viajero inmovil*.

    6. "Epithalamium," in *The Captain's Verses*, trans. Donald D. Walsh. (New York, 1972), 131; hereafter cited in text.

    7. Felstiner, "A Feminist Reading," 93.

    8. *Cien sonetos de amor* (Buenos Aires: Losada, 1971). English translations when indicated come from *Pablo Neruda: A New Decade, Poems 1958–1967*, trans. Ben Belitt and Alastair Reid (New York, 1969). Other translations of the Losada edition by Lorraine Roses.

    9. Belitt and Reid, *Pablo Neruda*, xxi.

    10. As mentioned before, this poem has not been carefully studied by critics. To the present the most informative article is by Fernando Alegría, *"La Barcarola:* Barca de la vida," *Revista Iberoamericana*, 39, nos. 82–83 (January–June):73–98.

Chapter Three

    1. For further information on the relationship of Spanish-American Modernism and the European avant-garde see the following books: Octavio Paz, *Los hijos del Limo* (Barcelona: Seix Barral, 1974) and *El caracol y la sirena* (The siren and the seashell) (Austin, Texas: University of Austin Press, 1976). Also for particular studies on Neruda's avant-garde works see, Lucía Guerra Cunningham, *"El habitante y su esperanza:* Primer exponente vanguardista en la novela chilena," *Hispania* 60 (1977):470–77,

and Jaime Alazraki, "El surrealismo de *Tentativa del hombre infinito* de Pablo Neruda," *Hispanic Review* 40 (1972):31–39.

2. Saul Yurkievich, *Fundadores de la nueva poesía latinoamericana* (Barcelona, 1971), 153.

3. René de Costa, *The Poetry of Pablo Neruda* (Cambridge, Mass, 1979), 44.

4. For this chapter we will use *Residence on Earth,* trans. Donald D. Walsh (New York, 1973).

5. Pablo Neruda and Hector Eandi, *Correspondencia durante "Residencia en la tierra,"* ed. Margarita Aguirre (Buenos Aires: Editorial Sud-Americana, 1980), 20.

6. Ibid., 45.

7. Ibid., 46.

8. Alonso's book *(Poesía y estilo de Pablo Neruda: Interpretación de una poesía hermética* [Buenos Aires, 1940]) is the point of departure for the linguistic and stylistic analysis of *Residencia en la tierra* and is followed by Alfredo Lozada, *El monismo agónico de Pablo Neruda: Estructura, significado y filiación de "Residencia en la tierra"* (México 1971). Also see the special issue dedicated to *Residence on Earth* in *Review '74* [Center for Inter-American Relations] (Spring 1974).

9. For further information on this journal, see Carmen Vazquez, "Pablo Neruda y *Caballo verde para la poesía,*" *Revista de Estudios Hispanicos* [Puerto Rico] 8 (1981); 55–68.

10. "Towards an Impure Poetry," in *Five Decades of Poems,* trans. Ben Belitt (New York, 1974), xxi.

11. See the study on *Residence on Earth* in Rodríguez Monegal, *El viajero inmovil,* and the book by Jaime Concha, *Pablo Neruda 1904-1936* (Santiago de Chile, 1972). Also by Jaime Concha, "Observaciones sobre algunas imagenes de *Residencia en la tierra,*" in Levy and Loveluck, eds., *Simposio Pablo Neruda: Actas,* 107–22.

12. Durán, *Earth Tones,* 42.

13. For further study on "Tres cantos materiales" see the article by Clarence Finlayson, "Pablo Neruda en 'Tres cantos materiales,' " in *Anales de la Universidad de Chile* 129 nos. 157–60, (January–December 1971):257–63.

14. For further comparative studies it would be interesting to examine the experience of César Vallejo and Pablo Neruda during the Civil War. For more information, see Marlene Gottlieb, "La Guerra Civil española en la poesía de Pablo Neruda y César Vallejo," *Cuadernos Americanos* 54 (1967):189–200. And also see Alfredo Lozada, "La interpretación socio-político de *Residencia en la tierra,*" *Journal of Inter-American Studies* 8 (April 1966):269–78.

Chapter Four

1. Alonso Ercilla y Zuñiga, *La Araucana*, ed. Abraham Koñig (Santiago: Imprenta Cervantes, 1888). For further study on *La Araucana* see Fernando Alegría, *La Poesia chilena: Origenes y desarollo del siglo XVI al XIX* (Los Angeles: University of California Press, 1953).

2. Rodríguez Monegal, *El viajero inmóvil*, 235.

3. Fernando Alegría, prologue to *Canto general* (Venezuela: Ediciones Ayacucho, 1970), 5.

4. Ibid., 6.

5. Eduardo Comacho, *Pablo Neruda: Naturalezan historia y poetica* (Madrid, 1978).

6. *Canto general* (Barcelona: Brugera, 1980), 325; hereafter cited in text.

7. Hernán Loyola, *Pablo Neruda: Propuesta de lectura* (Madrid, 1981), 220.

8. This information about the importance of Neruda's visit to Macchu Picchu appears in Margarita Aguirre's biography, *Las vidas*, 1973. This quotation from Neruda also reveals an orphic mission of the poet and his fellow man. For further analysis of this aspect see: Hernán Loyola, "Neruda y América Latina," *Cuadernos Americanos* 218 (1978):175–97 and also Jean Franco, "Orfeo en utopia: El poeta y la colectividad en el *Canto general*," in Levy and Loveluck, eds., *simposio Pablo Neruda: Actas*, 267–90.

9. de Costa, *The Poetry of Pablo Neruda*, 107.

10. Yurkievich, *Fundadores*, 156. Also see "Mito e historia: dos generadores del *Canto general*," *Revista Iberoamericana* 39, nos. 82–83 (June 1973): 111–35.

11. *The Heights of Macchu Picchu*, Nathaniel Tarn (New York, 1966), 2; hereafter cited in text. For further study on *The Heights of Macchu Picchu* see Cedomil Goić: " 'Las alturas de Macchu Picchu': La torre y el abismo," *Anales de la Universidad de Chile* 129, nos. 157–60 (January–December 1971): 153–65. Also, Juan Larrea, *Del surrealismo a Macchu Picchu* (Mexico, 1967).

12. For more information about the symbolism of the tree in the *Canto general* see the book by Frank Riess, *The Word and the Stone: Language and Imagery in Neruda's "Canto general"* (London and New York, 1972).

13. For the information concerning the caricaturesque element in the *Canto general* see Juan Vilegas, "El mundo demoniáco de América y los antiheroes: El bestiario de *Canto general*," in *Estructuras míticas y arquetípicas en el "Canto General" de Neruda* (Barcelona, 1976).

14. For further study on this section, see Saul Yurkievich, "El genésis oceánico," in Levy and Loveluck eds., *Simposio Pablo Neruda: Actas*, 383–401.

15. The critical bibliography on *Canto general* is extensive. I will mention the articles I have found useful for a global understanding. See Mireya Camurati, "Significación de *Canto general* en la obra de Pablo Neruda," *Revista Interamericana* 2, no. 2 (1972):210–22. Luis A. Diez, "Grandeza telúrica y aliento épico del *Canto general*," *Sin Nombre* 4, no 2 (1973):9–22. Sonja Karsen, "Neruda's *Canto general* in Historical Context,"*Symposium* 32 (1978):220–35. Nelson Osorio, "El problema del hablante poético en *Canto general*," in *Simposio Pablo Neruda: Actas*.

Chapter Five

1. The quotations of this edition are from *Memoirs,* trans. Hardie St. Martin.

2. *Passions and Impressions,* trans. Margaret Sayer Peden (New York: Farrar, Straus & Giroux, 1981).

3. All the quotations are from *Isla Negra: A Notebook,* trans. Alastair Reid (New York, 1970).

4. Ben Belitt, introduction to *Pablo Neruda.*

5. For further study concerning this important book *Memorial de Isla Negra* we suggest the following: Luis González-Cruz, *Memorial de Isla Negra: Integración de la visión poética de Pablo Neruda* (Miami, 1972) and a condensed article, by the same author, about the book, "Pablo Neruda: soledad, incomunicación e individualismo en *Memorial de Isla Negra,*" *Revista Iberoamericana* 39, nos. 82–83 (January–June 1973):245–62.

Chapter Six

1. This information is taken from Jaime Alazraki, "Observaciones sobre la estructura de la oda elemental," *Mester* 4, no. 2 (April 1974):102. Also for a detailed study of the structure of the *Odes* see, David Barry, "Sobre la 'Oda a Juan Tarrea,' " *Cuadernos Americanos* 159 (1968):197–214. And Jaime Alazraki, "Pablo Neruda: The Chronicler of All Things," *Books Abroad* 46 (1972):49–54.

2. "La casa de las odas," in *Obras Completas* (Buenos Aires: Losada, 1958), 88. Translation by Lorraine Roses.

3. "Ode to an Onion," in *Elementary Odes of Pablo Neruda,* trans. Carlos Lozano (New York, 1961), 126. All further quotations unless otherwise indicated will come from this edition.

4. Fernando Alegria, introduction to *Elementary Odes of Pablo Neruda,* 14.

5. de Costa, *The Poetry of Pablo Neruda,* 158. Also see the article by Vivianee Lerner, "Realité profane, réalité sacrée dans les *Odas Elementales* de Pablo Neruda," *Bulletin de la Faculté des Lettres de Strasbourg* 44 (1966):759–76, which also includes an analysis of the structural forms of the *Odes.*

6. *Toward the Splendid City,* 22.

7. "Oda al hombre sencillo," in *Pablo Neruda antología escencial* (Santiago: Nascimento, 1968), 169; hereafter cited in text.

8. Violeta Parra, "Gracias a la vida," in *Antología general* (Santiago: Editorial Aconcagua, 1977), 203.

9. *Extravagaria,* trans. Alastair Reid (New York, 1974); hereafter cited in text.

10. For further study dealing with the relationship of Nicanor Parra and Pablo Neruda, see the article by José Miguel Ibánez Langlois, "Parra y Neruda," in *Poesía chilena e hispanoamericana contemporánea* (Santiago: Editorial Nascimento, 1975) and the essay on Neruda by Parra in *Pablo y Nicanor Parra: Discursos* (Santiago: Editorial Nascimento, 1962).

11. David P. Gallagher, *Modern Latin American Literature* (London: Oxford University Press, 1973), 65.

Chapter Seven

1. At present, there are few articles about Neruda's posthumous work. The most interesting ones are those that speak of his silence and introspection, for example, Jaime Alazraki, "Para una poética de la poesía postúma en Pablo Neruda," in *Pablo Neruda,* eds. Emir Rodríquez Monegal and Enrique Mario Santí (Madrid, 1980), 283–310. Also, "Poética de la penumbra en la poesía más reciente de Pablo Neruda," *Revista Iberomericana* 39, nos. 82–83, (January–June 1973):262–92.

2. "Todos a saber," in *Jardín de invierno* (Barcelona: Seix Barral, 1974), 33; hereafter cited in text.

3. "Los Hombres IV," in *La rosa separada* (Buenos Aires: Losada, 1974), 27; hereafter cited in text.

4. See Dufan and Safir, *Earth Tones,* in the chapter dedicated to the posthumous poetry and the article of Jaime Alazraki, "Para una poética de la poesía postúma."

5. *El mar y las campanas* (Buenos Aires: Losada, 1974); hereafter cited in text.

6. *El libro de las preguntas* (Buenos Aires: Losada, 1974); hereafter cited in text. See also by Fernando Alegría, "Las preguntas de Neruda," *American Hispanist* 2, no. 12 (1976): 3–5.

Chapter Eight

1. For material on the childhood of Neruda, see Hamilton, *Pablo Neruda.* About Neruda's years in Valparaíso, see Sara Vial, *Neruda en Valparaíso* (Valparaíso, 1982).

2. Durán and Safir, *Earth Tones,* 12.

3. Enrico Mario Santí, *Pablo Neruda: The Poetics of Prophecy* (Ithaca, 1982), 6.

4. Juan Villegas, *Estructuras míticas y arquetípicas en el "Canto general,"* 43; translation by Lorraine Roses.

5. Ibid., 10.

6. A study that reviews superficially Neruda criticism is René Jara, "La crítica ante Neruda," *Chasqui* 7, no. 1 (1978): 56–62.

7. Complete bibliographic information on these texts appears in the bibliography of this book.

8. For further information on the influence of Neruda on North American poetry, see Emma Marras, "Robert Bly's Reading of South American Poets: A Challenge to North American Poetic Practice," *Translation Review*, no. 141 (1984): 33–39. See also Bly's work in Robert Bly and James Wright, trans., *Neruda and Vallejo: Selected Poems* (Boston: Beacon Press, 1972).

9. All books cited in translation appear in the bibliography.

10. For a very thorough study of the translations of Neruda into English since 1946, see John Felstiner, *Translating Neruda: The Way to Macchu Picchu* (Stanford, 1980), 13–25.

11. *Review '74* (Spring): 22. In the same issue see the article that attacks Walsh's theory of translation, "The Translator as Nobody in Particular," 23–28. For further information on theories of translation of Belitt, see *Adam's Dream: A Preface to Translation* (New York, 1978).

12. Gilbert, *Seven Voices,* 35–36 and the comment on Alastair Reid in the prologue to *Isla Negra: A Notebook.*

13. H. R. Hays, *The Heights of Macchu-Picchu,"* *Tiger's Eye,* 20 (October 1948), 112–21.

14. Gilbert, *Seven Voices,* 37.

Selected Bibliography

PRIMARY SOURCES

1. Original Editions

La canción de la fiesta. Santiago: Ediciones Juventud, 1921.

*Crepusculario.*Santiago: Editorial Claridad, 1923.

Veinte poemas de amor y una canción desesperada. Santiago: Nascimento, 1924.

*Anillos.*With Tomás Lago. Santiago: Nascimento, 1926.

El habitante y su esperanza. Santiago: Nascimento, 1926.

Tentativa del hombre infinito. Santiago: Nascimento, 1926.

El hondero entusiasta. Santiago: Empresa Letras, 1933.

Residencia en la tierra (1925–1931). Santiago: Nascimento, 1933.

Residencia en la tierra (1925–1935). 2 vols. Madrid: Cruz y Raya, 1935.

Tercera residencia (1935–1945). Buenos Aires: Editorial Losada, 1947.

Canto general. Mexico: Ediciones Océano, 1950.

Los versos del capitán. Naples: L'Arte tipografica, 1952.

Los versos del capitán. Buenos Aires: Editorial Losada, 1953.

Odas elementales. Buenos Aires: Editorial Losada, 1954.

Las uvas y el viento. Santiago: Nascimento, 1954.

Viajes. Santiago: Nascimento, 1955.

Nuevas odas elementales. Buenos Aires: Editorial Losada, 1956.

Tercer libro de las odas. Buenos Aires: Editorial Losada, 1957.

Estravagaria. Buenos Aires: Editorial Losada, 1958.

Cien sonetos de amor. Buenos Aires: Editorial Losada, 1959.

Navegaciones y regresos (Cuarto libro de las odas). Buenos Aires: Editorial Losada, 1959.

Canción de gesta. Havana: Imprenta Nacional de Cuba, 1960.

Cantos ceremoniales. Buenos Aires: Editorial Losada, 1961.

Las piedras de Chile. With photographs by Antonio Quintana. Buenos Aires: Editorial Losada, 1961.

Discursos. With Nicanor Parra. Santiago: Nascimento, 1962.

Plenos poderes. Buenos Aires: Editorial Losada, 1962.

Memorial de Isla Negra. Buenos Aires: Editorial Losada, 1964.

Romeo y Julieta. Translation of the work of William Shakespeare. Buenos Aires: Editorial Losada, 1964.

Arte de pajaros. Santiago: Sociedad de Amigos del Arte Contemporáneo, 1966.

144

Una casa en la arena. Barcelona: Lumen, 1966.

Barcarola. Buenos Aires: Editorial Losada, 1967.

Fulgor y muerte de Joaquín Murieta. Santiago: Zig-Zag, 1967.

Las manos del día. Buenos Aires: Editorial Losada, 1968.

Aún. Santiago: Nascimento, 1969.

Comiendo en Hungría. Barcelona: Lumen, 1969.

Fin del mundo. Santiago: Sociedad de Arte Contemporáneo, 1969.

La espada encendida. Buenos Aires: Editorial Losada, 1970.

Las piedras del cielo. Buenos Aires: Editorial Losada, 1970.

Geografía infructuosa. Buenos Aires: Editorial Losada, 1972.

La rosa separada. Buenos Aires: Editorial Losada, 1972.

Incitación al nixoncidio y alabanza de la revolución chilena. Santiago: Quimantú, 1973.

El mar y las campanas. Buenos Aires: Editorial Losada, 1973.

Confieso que he vivido: Memorias. Buenos Aires: Editorial Losada, 1974.

El corazón amarillo. Buenos Aires: Editorial Losada, 1974.

Defectos escogidos. Buenos Aires: Editorial Losada, 1974.

Elegía. Buenos Aires: Editorial Losada, 1974.

Libro de las preguntas. Buenos Aires: Editorial Losada, 1974.

Para nacer he nacido. Barcelona: Seix Barral, 1978.

El río invisible. Barcelona: Seix Barral, 1980.

2. Complete Editions

Poesías completas. Buenos Aires: Editorial Losada, 1951.

Obras completas. Buenos Aires: Editorial Losada, 1957.

Obras completas. 2d ed. Buenos Aires: Editorial Losada, 1962.

Obras completas. 3d ed. Edited by Margarita Aguirre; bibliography by
Alfonso M. Escudero and Hernán Loyola. Buenos Aires: Editorial
Losada, 1968.

Obras completas. 4th ed. Edited by Margarita Aguirre, Alfonso M. Escudero,
and Hernán Loyola. Buenos Aires: Editorial Losada, 1973.

3. Anthologies and Collections

Selección. Compiled and with notes by Arturo Aldunate. Santiago: Nascimento, 1943.

Obras poéticas. Compiled and with notes by Juvencio Valle. 10 vols. Santiago: Cruz del Sur, 1947–48.

Poesía política. Compiled by Margarita Aguirre. Santiago: Editorial Austral,
1953.

Todo el amor. Santiago: Nascimento, 1953.

Antología esencial. Compiles by Hernán Loyola. Buenos Aires: Editorial
Losada, 1971.

4. English Translations

A Call for the Destruction of Nixon and Praise for the Chilean Revolution.
Translated by Teresa Anderson. Cambridge, Mass.: West End Press,
1980.

The Captain's Verses. Translated by Donald D. Walsh. New York: New
Directions, 1972.

The Elementary Odes of Pablo Neruda. Translated by Carlos Lozano. New
York: Cypress, 1961.

Extravagaria. Translated by Alastair Reid. New York: Farrar, Straus and
Giroux, 1974.

Five Decades of Poems: A Selection. Translated by Ben Belitt. New York:
Grove Press, 1974.

The Heights of Macchu Picchu. Translated by Nathaniel Tarn. New York:
Farrar, Straus & Giroux, 1967.

Isla Negra: A Notebook. Translated by Alastair Reid. New York: Farrar,
Straus and Giroux, 1970.

Memoirs. Translated by Hardie St. Martin. New York: Farrar, Straus &
Giroux, 1977.

New Poems: 1968–1970. Translated by Ben Belitt. New York: Grove Press,
1972.

Residence on Earth. Translated by Donald D. Walsh. New York: New
Directions, 1973.

Residence on Earth and Other Poems. Translated by Angel Flores. Norfolk,
Conn.: New Directions, 1946.

Selected Poems: A Bilingual Edition. Edited by Nathaniel Tarn. Translated
by Anthony Kerrigan, W. S. Merwin, Alastair Reid, and Nathaniel
Tarn. New York: Delacorte Press, Seymour Lawrence, 1972.

Splendor and Death of Joaquin Murieta. Translated by Ben Belitt. New York:
Farrar, Straus & Giroux, 1972.

Twenty Love Poems and a Song of Despair. Translated by W. S. Merwin.
New York: Penguin Books, 1983.

SECONDARY SOURCES

1. *Books*

Aguirre, Margarita. *Las vidas de Pablo Neruda.* Santiago de Chile: Zig-
Zag, 1967. This biography, by Neruda's niece, is the most comprehensive to date. It reveals the sources of inspiration of many of Neruda's books.

Alazraki, Jaime.*Poetica y poesia de Pablo Neruda.* New York: Las Américas,
1965. One of the earliest critical studies on Neruda, this book examines the relation between Neruda and the French-inspired avant-

garde movement and analyzes in detail *Tentativa del hombre infinito* and *El habitante y su esperanza*.

Alonso, Amado. *Poesía y estilo de Pablo Neruda: Interpretación de una poesía hermética*. Buenos Aires: Losada, 1940. A pioneering study that examines in great detail the poetic discourse and the themes of the *Residences*, defined by Alonso as a "poetics of disintegration." This is the most detailed of the stylistic studies on the *Residences*. It analyzes meticulously the syntax, the rhythm, and the images of the two volumes. Alonso's study is the most famous example of form and content stylistics Hispanic literary criticism.

Belitt, Ben. *Adam's Dream: A Preface to Translation*. New York: Grove Press, 1978. Contains two chapters dedicated to the process and experience of translating Neruda, as well as a provocative essay on *Confieso que he vivido (Memoirs)* in which Belitt compares it to a prose epic valuable for its broad scope.

Bizarro, Salvatore. *Pablo Neruda: All the Poets, the Poet*. New Jersey: Scarecrow Press, 1979. This book studies Neruda's political and social poetry and contains interviews with Delia del Carril, Neruda's second wife, and Matilde Urrutia, Neruda's widow. It also includes a useful chapter on the *Memoirs*.

Camacho Guizado, Eduardo. *Pablo Neruda: Naturaleza, historia y poética*. Madrid: Sociedad General, Española de librería, 1978. A general introduction to the major books and themes of Neruda's poetry.

Concha, Jaime. *Pablo Neruda 1904-1936*. Santiago de Chile: Editorial Universitaria, 1972. A study that examines Neruda's life and poetry from a Marxist perspective. It also contains informative references to the historical and political events in Chile during Neruda's youth.

de Costa, René. *The Poetry of Pablo Neruda*. Cambridge, Mass. Harvard University Press, 1979. Thematic study of the major books by Neruda, with emphasis on the duality of consistency and change that is found in his poetry.

Durán, Manuel and Margery Safir. *Earth Tones*. Bloomington: Indiana University Press, 1980. A major study based on the recurrent themes in Neruda's poetry and poetics.

Felstiner, John. *Translating Neruda: The Way to Macchu Picchu*. Stanford: Stanford University Press, 1980. This book is particularly important since it sheds light on the creative process of translation. Felstiner adds important theoretical discussions on translation and the role of the translator. This significant monograph deals with the whole problematics of translation and cross-cultural interpretation.

Flores, Angel. *Aproximaciones a Pablo Neruda*. Barcelona: Libres de Sinera, 1974. A collection of critical studies on various aspects of Neruda's work.

Gilbert, Rita. *Seven Voices.* New York: Alfred A. Knopf, 1973. A lively portrait of the poet at his Isla Negra home.

González-Cruz, Luis E. *"Memorial de Ilsa Negra": Integración de la visión poética de Pablo Neruda.* Miami: Ediciones Universal, 1972. A definitive and detailed study that concentrates on thematic analysis of the five books included in *Memorial,* with emphasis on the aspect of recollection and memory.

————. *De tentativa a la totalidad.* New York: Ediciones Abra, 1983. The first study to analyze in detail *Tentativa* and its link to the French symbolists and surrealists.

Hamilton, Carlos. *Pablo Neruda: Poeta chileno universal.* Santiago de Chile: Lord Cochrane, 1972. A general study of Neruda's works, with emphasis on his attachment to the Chilean geography.

Larrea, Juan. *Del surrealismo a Macchu Picchu.* México: Joaquín Mortiz, 1967. Essays on Neruda and surrealism, including poetic and philosophical reflections on Neruda's experience at Macchu Picchu and the city itself as a symbol of Spanish-American culture.

Loyola, Hernán. *Ser y morir en Pablo Neruda, 1918-1945.* Santiago de Chile: Editorial Santiago, 1967. An important book, both concise and informative, that treats the early lyrical poems, up until the time of Neruda's conversion to Marxism.

————. *Pablo Neruda: Propuesta de lectura.* Madrid: Alianza Editorial, 1981. This book contains the prologues, written by Loyola, to his *Antología poética de Pablo Neruda.* In them Loyola summarizes the phases of Neruda's poetic development from 1915 to 1973. Especially interesting is the final chapter, which treats the seclusion of Neruda.

Lozada, Alfredo. *El monismo agónico de Pablo Neruda: Estructura, significado y filiación de "Residencia en la tierra."* México: B. Costa Amic., 1971. Detailed thematic and stylistic analysis of *Residence on Earth.* Taking as point of departure Amado Alonso's seminal study, Lozada makes the *Residences* more accessible to the general reader and clarifies the obscure imagery of this work.

Montes, Hugo. *Para leer a Neruda.* Buenos Aires: Editorial Francisco de Aguirre, 1975. Useful general introduction to Neruda and criticism on Neruda.

Osorio, Nelson and Fernando Moreno. *Claves de Pablo Neruda.* Valparaíso: Ediciones Universidad de Valparaíso, 1971. Bibliography of works by and about Neruda.

Riess, Frank. *The Word and the Stone: Language and Imagery in Neruda's "Canto general."* London and New York: Oxford University Press, 1972. Major study of the poetic and symbolic imagination of *Canto general.* Emphasis on the explication of Neruda's recurrent images such as the tree and the stone.

Rodríguez Monegal, Emir. *El viajero inmóvil, introduccion a Pablo Neruda.* Buenos Aires: Losada, 1966. A pioneering literary biography of Neruda with insightful comments on the personal experiences of the poet and their manifestation in his work.

————. and Enrico Mario Santí. *Pablo Neruda.* Madrid: Taurus, 1980. A collection of essays on various aspects of Neruda as well as testimonial essays by many of Neruda's friends.

Santí, Enrico Mario. *Pablo Neruda: The Poetics of Prophecy.* Ithaca: Cornell University Press, 1982. A study of the prophetic motif in Neruda's work, especially in the *Canto general* and its roots in the Western literary tradition.

Sicard, Alain. *El pensamiento poético de Pablo Neruda.* Madrid: Gredos, 1983. A major study dedicated to the philosophical and metaphysical concepts found in Neruda's poetry.

Suárez Rivero, Eliana. *El gran amor de Pablo Neruda: Estudio critico de su poesía.* Madrid: Ediciones Plaza Mayor, 1971. One of the early studies of the love poetry by Neruda.

Vial, Sara. *Neruda en Valparaíso.* Valparaíso: Ediciones Universidad de Valparaíso, 1982. Journalistic book, with photographs, on the time Neruda spent in the coastal city of Valparaíso.

Villegras, Juan. *Estructuras miticas y arquetipos en el "Canto general" de Neruda.* Barcelona: Editorial Planeta, 1976. Concise analysis of the mythical and archetypal images found in *Canto general,* with special emphasis on the concept of the mythical hero.

Yurkiévich, Saúl. *Fundadores de la nueva poesia latinoamericana: Huidobro, Borges, Neruda y Paz.* Barcelona: Barral Editores, 1971, especially 163–222, 223–52. Yurkiévich explores the workings of Neruda's cosmic and mythologic imagination arguing that his poetic inspiration develops out of an intuitive grasp of the world around him.

2. *Selected Articles*

Alazraki, Jaime. "Pablo Neruda: The Chronicle of All Things." *Books Abroad* 46 (1972):49–54. An overview of the *Odes,* with emphasis on the technique by which Neruda gives life to inanimate objects.

————. "El surrealismo de *Tentativa del hombre infinito.*" *Hispanic Review* 40 (1972):31–39. A summary of the main currents of surrealism and the influence of Bréton on Neruda.

————. "Music as Silence in Neruda's Eight Post-Books of Poetry." *Books Abroad* 50 (1976):40–45. Analysis of the technique of conveying sound and silence in the posthumous poetry.

————. "Punto de vista y recodificación en los poemas de 'Autoexégesis' de Pablo Neruda." *Symposium* 32 (1978):184–97. Exploration of Ner-

uda's poetics, based on the word of Neruda himself, in lectures and
in the *Memoirs*.

Alegría, Fernando. "Las preguntas de Neruda." *American Hispanist* 2, 12
(1976):3–5. Analysis that categorizes the different questions posed
by Neruda in *El libro de las preguntas*.

Barry, David. "Sobre la 'Oda a Juan Larrea.' " *Cuadernos Americanos* 159
(1968):197–214. A close reading of the stylistics of the Nerudian
ode, as a more complex and dynamic concept than that of the classical
ode.

Camurati, Mireya. "Significación de *Canto general* en la obra de Pablo
Neruda." *Revista Interamericana* 2, no. 2 (1972):210–22. Discusses
the social, political, and historical dimensions of the *Canto general*.

Ciorda Muguerza, Javier. "Neruda: Teoría y práxis poética." *Ceiba* [Puerto
Rico] 7, no. 12 (August–December 1983):31–43. Innovative study
that illuminates Neruda's poetics as seen in his major books.

Concha, J. "Neruda: 'La tierra se llama Pablo.' " *Nova* [Lisbon] 1976:114–
19. Essay on the death of the poet, his Chilean childhood, and his
adherence to Marxism.

———— "Los origenes de la primera infancia de Neruda." *Revista Iberoam-*
ericana 36 (1971):389–406. A seminal artical on the *Residences*. Concha studies in detail the images and symbols of these books as well
as the metaphysical content implicit in it.

————. "Interpretación de *Residencia en la tierra*." *Mapocho* 2 (July 1963):5–
39. One of the most comprehensive articles on the *Residences*. Concha
studies in detail the images and symbols of these books as well as
the metaphysical content implicit in them.

de Costa René. "Sobre Huidobro y Neruda." *Revista Iberoamericana,* nos.
106–7 (January–June 1979):379–86. A study of the polemics between Huidobro and Neruda, with valuable quotes that reveal the
poets' thoughts about themselves and each other.

Diez, Luis A. "Grandeza telúrica y aliento épico del *Canto general*." *Sin
Nombre* 4, no. 2 (1973):9–22. Emphasizes the language and the
telluric imagination of the *Canto general*.

Durán, Manuel. "Pablo Neruda y la tradición romántica y simbolica."
Cuadernos Americanos 3 (1980:197–99. General overview that situates
Neruda as heir to the romantic tradition of the nineteenth century,
especially that of Baudelaire, Rimbaud, and Mallarmé.

Droguett, Iván. "Apuntes sobre 'Fulgor y muerte de Joaquín Murieta' de
Pablo Neruda." *Latin American Theatre Review* 2, no. 1 (1968):39–
48. Innovative study on the themes and theatrical elements of Neruda's play "Fulgor y muerte de Joaquín Murieta."

Engler, Kay. "Image and Structure in Neruda's *Las alturas de Macchu Picchu.* *Symposium* 27, no. 2 (1974):130–45. Concise close reading of the thematic unities of *The Heights of Macchu Picchu.*

Felstiner, John. "A Feminist Reading of Neruda". *Parnassus: Poetry in Review* 3, no. 2 (1974):90–112. Felstiner concludes that in Neruda's love poetry, especially *Twenty Love Poems* and *One Hundred Sonnets,* woman is treated both as muse and as sex object.

————. "Translating Pablo Neruda's 'Galope Muerto.' " PMLA 93 (1978):208–20. Felstiner, a fine translator, analyzes in detail his experience translating this important poem from the first *Residence.*

Finlayson, Clarence. "Pablo Neruda en 'Tres cantos materiales.' " *Anales de la Universidad de Chile* (January–December 1971):157–60. Detailed critical analysis of the poems "Entrada a la madera" and "Tres cantos materiales."

Forster, Merlin H. "Pablo Neruda and the Avant-Garde." *Symposium* 32 (1978):208–20. Forster follows the main threads of Neruda's poetry and his personality. He argues that Neruda never really took part in the avant-garde, but was an "independent poet."

Goić, Cedomil. *"Las alturas de Macchu Picchu:* La torre y el abismo." *Anales de la Universidad de Chile* (January–December 1971):153–67. Excellent analysis of *Las alturas de Macchu Picchu* and the mythical quest of the hero. Goić dedicates several sections to the recurrent motif of death.

González-Cruz, Luis F. "El viaje transcendente de Pablo Neruda: Una lectura de *Tentativa del hombre infinito.*" *Symposium* 32 (1978):197–208. Centers on the motif of the nocturnal and mystical voyage found in this poem.

Gottlieb, Marlene. "La Guerra Civil española en la poesía de Pablo Neruda y César Vallejo." *Cuadernos Americanos* 54 (1967):189–200. A thematic comparison of the similarity and divergences between these two poets who witnessed the Spanish Civil War.

Karsen, Sonja. "Neruda's *Canto general* in Historical Context." *Symposium* 32 (1978):220–35. An introductory study that stresses the relationship between historical facts, politics, and fiction in the *Canto.*

Lavín Cerda, Hernán. "Pablo Neruda o la cornucopia del animal oscuro." *Cuadernos Americanos* 252 (January–February 1984):111–28. An important article that brings together Neruda's ideas on poetry and the act of writing.

Loyola, Hernán. "Lectura de *Veinte poemas de amor.*" In *Simposio Pablo Neruda: Actas,* edited by Isaac J. Lévy and J. Loveluck, 339–54. New York: Las Americas, 1975. A detailed study of the autobiographical story behind the creation of *Twenty Poems* and of its principal symbols.

———. "El ciclo nerudiano 1958–1967." *Anales de la Universidad de Chile* ("Estudios sobre Pablo Neruda")129, nos. 157–60 (January-December 1971):235–54. Analysis of the themes and styles of Neruda during this period. Loyola points out the importance of Matilde Urrutia at this juncture of Neruda's life.

Osorio, Nelson. "El problema del hablante poético en *Canto general.*" In *Simposio Pablo Neruda: Actas,* 171–88. A theoretical essay that analyzes the lyrical voices utilized in the *Canto general.*

Rodríguez Fernández, Mario. "La búsqueda del espacio feliz: La imagen de la casa en la poesía de Pablo Neruda." *Anales de la Universidad de Chile* 129, nos. 157–60 (January-December 1971):217–27. Unique study that develops the theme of domesticity in Neruda's poetry, indicating that in the poems that deal with this theme, the idea of "home" appears as a disorderly space without refuge.

Salmon, Russel and Julia Lesage. "Stones and Birds: Consistency and Change in Poetry of Pablo Neruda." *Hispania* 60, no. 2 (May 1977):224–41. A detailed analysis of the imagery found in two lesser known works of Neruda, *Las piedras de chile* and *Arte de los pajaros.* The authors argue that these two books present a dialectic materialism based on consistency and change.

Sicard, Alain. "Soledad, muerte y conciencia histórica en la poesía reciente de Pablo Neruda." In *Simposio Pablo Neruda. Actas,* 147–59. Study that traces the principal thematic coordinates in Neruda's poetry from 1958–70.

Valdivieso, Jaime. "Neruda: Misión y poesía." *Atenea,* 170, no. 4 (1968):421–36. Exploration of a Latin American conscientiousness in the poetry and the life of Neruda.

Yurkievich, Saul. "El génesis oceánico." In *Simposio Pablo Neruda: Actas,* 385–99. Detailed analysis of the main images found in the section of the *Canto general* entitled "El gran océano." Yurkievich states that there is a structural parallelism in the three "cantos" called, respectively, "La lámpara en la tierra," "Canto general de Chile" and "El gran oceano."

———. "Mito e historia: Dos generadores del *Canto general.*" *Revista Iberoamericana* 39, nos. 82–83 (June 1973):111–35. Here Yurkievich studies the imaginative consciousness of *Canto general* and its historical dimension.

3. *Special Magazine Issues*

Anales de Literatura Hispanoamericana [Madrid] 2, nos. 2–3 (1973–74). "Homenaje a Pablo Neruda y Miguel Angel Asturias."

Anales de la Universidad de Chile 129, nos. 157–60 (January–December 1971). "Estudios sobre Pablo Neruda."

Crisis [Buenos Aires], no. 2 (November 1973).

Insula [Madrid] 29 no. 330 (May 1974).

Modern Poetry Studies [Buffalo, NY] 5, no. 1 (Spring 1974). "Pablo Neruda, 1904–1973."

Review '74. [Center for Inter-American Relations] (Spring). "Focus/*Residence on Earth.*"

Revista Iberoamericana 39, nos. 82–83 (January–June 1973).

Simposio Pablo Neruda: Actas. Edited by I. J. Lévy and J. Loveluck. University of South Carolina-Las Américas. New York: Las Américas Publishing Co., 1975.

Index

a 861.42
N 454

118 813

DATE DUE

GAYLORD			PRINTED IN U.S.A.